Routledge Revivals

The Economics of Non-Wage Labour Costs

Throughout the OECD, 30% of the average firm's total labour costs comprises items which are other than direct remuneration. This reissue, first published in 1984, focuses upon these non-wage labour costs, which include: fringe-benefit payments, obligatory social-welfare contributions, holiday entitlements and expenditures on recruitment and training.

The book focuses on two major areas of enquiry: firstly, the costs for the cyclical behaviour of employment, and secondly, the role of average working hours per employee in the firm's overall allocation of labour services. The author begins with an empirical survey and costs breakdown, followed by extensive data on Japan, the UK, the USA and West Germany. The ensuing analysis considers the question as to why firms incur the various non-wages, and a comparative static factor demand model is constructed, which accommodates the major cost items.

The Economics of Non-Wage Labour Costs

Robert A. Hart

Routledge
Taylor & Francis Group

First published in 1984
by George Allen & Unwin Ltd

This edition first published in 2010 by Routledge
2 Park Square, Milton Park, Abingdon, Oxon, OX14 4RN

Simultaneously published in the USA and Canada
by Routledge
270 Madison Avenue, New York, NY 10016

Routledge is an imprint of the Taylor & Francis Group, an informa business

A Library of Congress record exists under ISBN: 0-04-331096-6

ISBN 13: 978-0-415-58942-0 (hbk)
ISBN 13: 978-0-203-84466-3 (ebk)

ISBN 10: 0-415-58942-8 (hbk)
ISBN 10: 0-203-84466-1 (ebk)

The Economics of Non-Wage Labour Costs

The Economics of Non-Wage Labour Costs

Robert A. Hart

London
GEORGE ALLEN & UNWIN
Boston Sydney

George Allen & Unwin (Publishers) Ltd,
40 Museum Street, London WC1A 1LU, UK

George Allen & Unwin (Publishers) Ltd,
Park Lane, Hemel Hempstead, Herts HP2 4TE, UK

Allen & Unwin, Inc.,
9 Winchester Terrace, Winchester, Mass. 01890, USA

George Allen & Unwin Australia Pty Ltd,
8 Napier Street, North Sydney, NSW 2060, Australia

First published in 1984

British Library Cataloguing in Publication Data

Hart, Robert A.
The economics of non-wage labour costs.
1. Costs, Industrial 2. Cost control
3. Personnel management
I. Title
658.1'553 HD47.5
ISBN 0-04-331096-6

Library of Congress Cataloging in Publication Data

Hart, Robert A.
The economics of non-wage labour costs.
1. Employee fringe benefits. 2. Labor costs.
I. Title.
HD4928.N6H37 1984 331.25'5 83-22328
ISBN 0-04-331096-6

Set in 10 on 11 point Times by MCS Ltd, Salisbury, Wilts, UK
and printed in Great Britain by
Biddles Ltd, Guildford, Surrey

Contents

For my mother
and in memory of
Margaret Buchanan

Acknowledgements

My main motivation for writing this book stems from the fact that I have recently been involved in a reasonably wide range of projects, most of which are ongoing, designed to examine the effects of non-wage labour costs on several aspects of labour market behaviour. In the course of undertaking this work, it seemed to be a worthwhile exercise to integrate the essential features of the whole subject area into a single text in an attempt to fill a gap in the labour market literature.

My first general interest in the subject stems from a study undertaken with David Bell and Frank Kirwan into non-wage labour costs in Italy, the United Kingdom and West Germany (*Non-Wage Labour Costs, their Importance and Effects*, Commission of the European Communities, 1980). Some of the work since then has also involved joint efforts. My co-researchers are Les Robb (on modelling endogenous non-wage labour costs), Alan Harrison (on the relationship between unemployment insurance contributions and the rate of unemployment), Felix FitzRoy (on unemployment insurance contributions and temporary layoffs) and Peter McGregor (on returns to factor inputs in the production function). I am grateful to all these colleagues for many stimulating discussions on these and related areas of work. From time to time throughout the text I make reference to my current research as well as to a number of very recently published papers. In this latter respect, I am grateful to the editors of *Oxford Economic Papers* and *Kyklos* for allowing me to reproduce some of the content of journal articles that are discussed, respectively, in Chapters 7 and 8.

I am grateful to the Science Centre, Berlin, for providing the funds and facilities for research into the book and also to the Director of the Institute of Labour Market Policy, Fritz Scharpf, for his encouragement and support of this work. Karl-Heinz Gatterdam and Ulla Regenhard provided competent research assistance, while Mitsuyasu Maeda (in particular), Yasushi Iguchi, Fred Lindsey, Jonathan Aldrich, Nagahisa Hiraishi, Herr Klaus Löning and Frau Lobinger were very helpful with queries over statistical information. While retaining all responsibility for errors and misconceptions, thanks are due to Frank Kirwan, Felix FitzRoy, Seiichi Kawasaki and Kanji Yamamoto who gave useful comments on parts of the book. I would also like to express my gratitude to Angelika Dierkes and Sylvia Pichorner for expert typing of earlier drafts and the final manuscript. Finally, I send my love to my wife Shirley and to Jennifer, Linsey and

Rosalind all of whom experienced non-wage costs during the last few months of writing the text.

Robert A. Hart
Science Centre
Berlin
May 1983

Preface

Non-wage labour costs are those categories of the firm's total labour costs that comprise other than direct remuneration and include fringe benefit payments, obligatory social welfare contributions, expenditures on recruitment and training as well as many other special cost items. They account for a very significant proportion of the firm's total expenditure on labour, averaging roughly 30 per cent of total labour costs throughout OECD countries. Moreover, since the early 1960s, many countries have experienced growth rates in non-wages that have exceeded both direct labour remuneration as well as labour productivity. Not only are such costs quantitatively important, but they also influence the firm's labour market behaviour in ways that are not captured by studies that concentrate primarily on the role of direct wages. Their two most important effects form the main areas of interest in this book. The first concerns the implications of the costs for the cyclical behaviour of employment, output and wages. The second deals with the essential role played by average working hours within the firm's labour services requirements given recognition of the costs.

The structure of the book is as follows. After a brief introduction on the subject area in Chapter 1, Chapters 2 and 3 provide details of the structure, quantitative importance and essential breakdowns of the costs. These are based on statistical information provided in four OECD countries, with the data organised in such a way as to attain the greatest possible comparability across countries. The countries are Japan, the United Kingdom, the United States and West Germany. The chapters have been purposely designed to provide the main statistical background for later developments in as succinct a manner as possible. Chapters 4 and 5 then play a pivotal role within the structure of the whole text. Chapter 4 asks why firms incur the range of costs indicated in the previous chapters. The relatively broad sweep of the chapter provides an ideal opportunity for highlighting what will be the main areas of interest at later stages in the book's development. Chapter 5 also deals with most aspects of the labour cost distinctions outlined earlier, but in a somewhat more technical manner. After setting out a general comparative static model, it examines the consequences of cost changes for factor substitution by analysing five simplified sub-model versions, each of which imposes a different set of constraints. Again, this chapter is specifically designed to provide a foreward link, since later sections draw quite heavily on the results obtained. The implications of non-wage costs for the cyclical behaviour of labour markets, particularly with respect to employment, are the subject of Chapter 6. This begins by examining the simplest model from Chapter 5 and then extends the discussion to cover three, more elaborate, related versions from the literature. Some empirical evidence is presented and a number of related topics are also discussed; the most important of these concerns returns to factor inputs in production theory. Chapter 7 is devoted to the subjects of wage inflation and wage rigidities. The wage inflation section deals with cyclical wage responsiveness and links closely with the developments in Chapters 5 and 6. In the section on wage rigidity, some relatively recent work is discussed that deals with the implications of certain types of non-wage for the firm's wage reactions in the face of unanticipated falls in product demand. Chapter 8 concentrates on one specific category of non-wages – obligatory, or statutory, social welfare payments – and its relation to layoffs and unemployment. Particular emphasis is given to the employment effects of changes in the firm's contributions to unemployment insurance and their relationship to the dominant supply-orientated literature. The potential implications of changes in non-wage costs for worksharing form the basis of discussion in Chapter 9. In particular, the chapter examines the feasibility of increasing the workforce and reducing average hours per worker through changes both in non-wages and in other related variables. Recently, an important literature has grown with respect to another major category of non-wage labour costs – fringe benefit payments. This has essentially concentrated on the question of why firms pay fringe benefits and Chapter 10 is devoted to reviewing the work critically within a unified framework. Finally, a brief policy discussion is undertaken in Chapter 11 with the intention of weighing up the reasons for and against government action to reduce non-wage labour costs to the firm.

The Economics of Non-Wage Labour Costs

1 Introduction

Non-wage labour costs (NWLCs) are those categories of the firm's total labour costs that comprise other than direct remuneration. They include fringe benefit payments, obligatory social welfare contributions, expenditures on recruitment and training as well as many other special cost items. Taken together, they form a very significant part of the average firm's total expenditure on labour. Table 1.1 shows, for all industries, the ratio of NWLCs to total labour costs in eight OECD countries from 1966 to 1981. In 1981, they averaged 25 – 40 per cent of the total. Further, while the ratios have increased somewhat since the mid-1960s, it is clear that throughout this period NWLCs averaged roughly 30 per cent of total labour costs for all countries.

Major interest in the influence of non-wage labour costs on labour market behaviour began in the early 1960s with the advent of important developments in human capital theory. This work concentrated primarily on investigating the effects of recruitment and training investments on the firm's cyclical demand for workers. Later contributions extended both the range of costs included in general labour market analysis as well as their scope of influence. Three explanations help to account for this somewhat late development of the subject area. First, NWLCs have a relatively short history of constituting a

Table 1.1 *Non-wage labour costs as a percentage of total labour costs: eight OECD countries, 1966 – 81*

Country	*1966*	*1972*	*1975*	*1978*	*1981*
Belgium	31.9	34.9	37.2	33.9	—
France	37.4	36.3	38.5	38.1	38.3
Italy	37.6	38.5	41.9	43.6	—
Japan	—[a]	—	18.3	23.2	—
Netherlands	32.4	35.7	39.5	34.2	34.2
United Kingdom	—	19.4[b]	22.9	26.8	29.3
United States	21.0	24.6	26.1	27.0	27.1
West Germany	27.2	29.6	32.9	32.7	33.7

[a] Not available.
[b] 1973.
Sources: see Table A 2.1.

major labour cost consideration to the firm. In most OECD countries, the foundations of social welfare programmes were not laid down until the Great Depression, and the associated payroll taxes on firms did not gain real significance until the postwar period (see, for example, US Chamber of Commerce, 1981).[1] Likewise, compensation in the form of fringe benefits and paid non-work activity did not feature as major labour cost items until after the early 1950s.[2] Second, statistical information on NWLCs has been, and continues to be, decidedly inferior to that on wages and other key labour market variables. However, particularly since the mid-1960s, a much wider and detailed systematic national coverage of the costs has become available, particularly in Europe and Japan. Third, it required two theoretical breakthroughs, both in the 1960s, before it was generally appreciated that NWLCs play a *unique role* in the firm's labour market behaviour and thus require special attention in their own right. It is largely on the ramifications of these two developments that this book concentrates.

The first of these breakthroughs was achieved, independently, by Oi (1962) and Becker (1964), who concentrated their attention on those non-wage labour costs that represent human capital investments by the firm. They were concerned primarily with the NWLCs involved in hiring, firing and training workers, but their analyses also offered explanations for the payment of certain types of private fringe benefits. The work generalised the standard classical theory of employment through its emphasis on the optimising firm's behaviour in the face of the fact that these types of NWLC, unlike wages, are largely *fixed* in the short run. Under the profit-maximising condition, treating labour as a quasi-fixed rather than as a variable factor of production has fundamental implications for the behaviour of the labour input variable, particularly in the event of unanticipated changes in product demand. Oi and Becker's contributions laid the basic foundations for a body of related work that investigated the cyclical relationships among employment, output and wages.

The second development was carried out by Rosen (1968), who established that differentiating between fixed and variable labour costs necessitated treating labour sevices as a function of both the stock of workers *and* its rate of utilisation (as measured by the average hours worked per worker). Again, the principal results here hinge on the fact that certain non-wages are per-worker costs. However, this was by no means a trivial extension to Oi and Becker since it established beyond doubt that studying labour market phenomena associated with changes in the labour input without differentiating between workers and hours per worker can produce seriously misleading inferences and results.

Table 1.2 *Changes in employment and average hours in Europe, Japan and the USA, 1974 – 7*[a]

Year	*Average of eight European countries*[b]		*Japan*		*USA*	
	Employment	*Average hours*	*Employment*	*Average hours*	*Employment*	*Average hours*
1974	0.3	−2.5	0.2	−4.5	−0.4	−1.5
1975	−3.9	−2.9	−5.1	−2.6	−8.6	−1.2
1976	−1.7	1.5	0.4	3.2	3.7	1.2
1977	−0.7	−0.4	−0.2	0.3	3.6	0.6

[a] All figures are rates of change computed from the least squares trend of the logarithms of the index numbers.
[b] France, Germany, Italy, UK, Belgium, Denmark, Netherlands, Sweden.
Source: P. Capdevielle and D. Alvarez (1981), 'International comparisons of productivity and labour costs', *Monthly Labor Review,* 104(12).

It is worth emphasising the importance of the workers–hours distinction, if only to defend the fact that it receives particularly strong attention throughout Chapters 5 – 11 of this text. Table 1.2 shows the changes (measured as deviations from trend) in manufacturing employment and average hours, in Europe, Japan and the USA for the periods during and immediately following the 1974/5 recession. From these figures it is clear that analysing the labour response only in terms of employment would misrepresent both the size and nature of the recessionary impact. In all countries, though particularly in Europe and Japan, the magnitude of the hours-adjustment response relative to that of employment is such that to concentrate attention solely on the latter would lead to a serious underestimate of the total labour response. Note also that the *timing* of the hours adjustment is quite different from that of employment. In general, hours changes appear to lead employment changes both in the initial economic downturn and in the subsequent upturn. Hall (1980) has broken down the labour effects of output changes (measured as percentage deviation from trend) in this and the 1970/1 recession in the USA and has shown that the decrease in work effort (output per hour and hours per worker) is equal in importance to decreases in employment and participation.

While, as will be seen later, the role of certain categories of NWLCs is consistent with the picture portrayed in Table 1.2, it is not the intention here to investigate actual causality. Rather, in support of the approach adopted in this book, the example is used to endorse Hall's claim that 'determination of the intensity of work and hours on the job is an issue just as important as determination of the total number of people at work or in the labor force' (Hall, 1980, p. 96).

Extensions of the Oi, Becker and Rosen work helped to broaden the scope of interest in non-wage labour costs. Three important examples are as follows. The conceptual parallel between the stock and utilisation of labour on the one hand and the capital stock and capacity utilisation on the other was brought to the fore by Nadiri and Rosen (1969). In particular, they achieved a notable advance in production and factor demand theory by investigating the full interrelatedness of the two dimensions of both factors. Ehrenberg (1971) extended the labour demand theory (and the accompanying econometric estimation) associated with NWLCs by broadening both the range of costs included in the system and the number of other related economic variables. A generalisation of the Oi/Becker framework was presented by Hashimoto (1975 and later work) to allow for the possibility of price-adjustment, as well as quantity-adjustment, reactions to unanticipated falls in product demand. These and other contributions are discussed in later chapters.

Essentially, the text falls into two, albeit highly related, parts. The structure and quantitative importance of non-wage labour costs are discussed in Chapters 2 and 3 with reference to published data on four of the countries in Table 1.1. These are Japan, the UK, the USA and West Germany (FRG). It should be emphasised that the prime aim of these two chapters is to provide a general statistical background to some of the topics of interest in later chapters. Only limited reference is made to the particular attributes of individual countries that help to explain a given national structure of costs. Chapters 4–10 then concentrate on the labour market analysis of NWLCs. In general, they deal both with the reasons why firms incur such costs and, more importantly, with the effects of the costs on firms' labour market behaviour, particularly in the areas of employment and wage determination. Chapter 11 presents some brief policy conclusions.

While the orientation of all chapters is towards non-wages as labour costs to the firm, this does not mean that the effects of non-wages on workers, who both receive and contribute to non-wage benefits, are ignored. In the chapters dealing with wage determination and unemployment, in particular, it is essential to accommodate supply-side issues. However, the overall emphasis is on costs rather than benefits. Further, it should be underlined that the approach adopted highlights short- rather than long-term effects. This helps to bring out the potential importance of changes in hours of work as an adjustment mode. It also necessitates the development of the firm's likely responses to payroll tax changes beyond those concerned with tax shifting.

NOTES

1 Little long-run data series on non-wage costs exist for OECD countries. However, the US Chamber of Commerce has systematically collected information on employer contributions to employee benefits in company surveys conducted since the late 1940s. The following table presents estimates for four postwar periods as well as for 1929. The estimates in the table are weighted more towards smaller companies than in the Chamber's regular surveys and also include rather more industries. Both factors serve to reduce the estimated benefit size relative to the regular surveys. However, they give an accurate representation of the main trends.

Estimated employee benefits as percentage of wages and salaries in the total US economy, 1929 – 79

Type of payment	*1929*	*1951*	*1961*	*1971*	*1979*
Legally required[a]	0.8	3.3	5.1	7.2	9.4
Agreed-upon[b]	0.4	2.7	4.6	5.9	8.1
Time not worked[c]	0.7	5.5	7.1	8.4	9.4

[a] Old age, survivor, disability and hospital insurance payments, unemployment compensation, worker's compensation, government employee retirement, other.
[b] Pensions, insurance, other.
[c] Vacation, holidays, sick leave, other.
Sources: Wages and salaries from US Department of Commerce; benefits estimated by US Chamber of Commerce: *Employee Benefits Historical Data, 1951–1979* (Washington, DC: Chamber of Commerce of the United States, 1981).

Thus in 1979, legally required company payments as a proportion of wages and salaries had increased ten-fold from 1929 and almost three-fold from 1951.

2 Again, some evidence to support this, particularly in the case of fringe benefits, is provided by the US figures in the table in note 1.

REFERENCES

Becker, G. S. (1964), *Human Capital: A Theoretical and Empirical Analysis, with Special Reference to Education,* New York, NY: National Bureau of Economic Research.

Capdevielle, P. and D. Alvarez (1981), 'International comparisons of productivity and labor costs', *Monthly Labor Review,* 104 (12).

Ehrenberg, R. G. (1971), *Fringe Benefits and Overtime Behavior,* Massachusetts: Heath & Co.

Hall, R. E. (1980), 'Employment fluctuations and wage rigidity', *Brookings Papers on Economic Activity,* 1, 91–124.

Hashimoto, M. (1975), 'Wage reduction, unemployment and specific human capital', *Economic Inquiry,* 13, 485–504.

Nadiri, M. I. and S. Rosen (1969), 'Interrelated factor demand functions', *American Economic Review,* 59, 457–471.

Oi, W. (1962), 'Labour as a quasi-fixed factor', *Journal of Political Economy,* 70, 538–555.

Rosen, S. (1968), 'Short-run employment variation on class-I railroads in the US, 1947–1963', *Econometrica,* 36, 511–529.

US Chamber of Commerce (1981), *Employee Benefits Historical Data, 1951–1979,* Washington, DC: Chamber of Commerce of the United States.

2 The Structure of Non-Wage Labour Costs: Definitions and Distinctions

This chapter has two main objectives. First, it describes the individual cost items to the firm that together constitute non-wage labour costs. The items are ordered into a set of broader categories that not only help to simplify definitions throughout the book but also facilitate the cross-country comparisons of costs undertaken in this and the subsequent chapters. Secondly, it highlights two important dichotomies of NWLCs that are of considerable relevance to the economic analysis of later chapters. These are the distinctions between endogenous and exogenous costs and between quasi-fixed and variable costs. An essential requirement to the latter distinction is some clarification of the system under which firms pay obligatory social welfare contributions, and this is also undertaken here. So as not to burden the main text with tedious detail, information on sources, individual country cost structures and sundry calculations are presented in an Appendix to the chapter.

2.1 GENERAL COST CLASSIFICATION

There is no standard classification on non-wage labour costs. The intention is to adopt the widest possible definition that embraces most of the labour costs faced by the firm other than direct remuneration. Direct labour costs, which from time to time will be referred to somewhat loosely as 'wage costs', include wages, salaries, premium payments, bonuses and other, relatively small, items. NWLC definitions in published statistical sources are often more narrowly based. For example, the *National Accounts* of the OECD include only firms' statutory payments to social welfare and voluntary contributions to private insurance schemes. The relatively rich data sources from which information is drawn for the four countries investigated here allow both more categories to be added and a somewhat more detailed subdivision of the constituent parts of each category. Since certain individual chapters, or sections of chapters, are geared to analysing

Table 2.1 *Classification of labour costs by EC standard*

Classification	*Content of the EC survey*
Wage costs:	
Direct remuneration and regular bonuses	Wages and salaries related to actual work – basic salaries and wages for normal and over-time hours – premiums and bonuses paid at each pay period
Other bonuses and gratuities	– Other premiums and bonuses not paid at each pay period
Payments to workers' savings schemes	Payments to workers' savings schemes
Non-wage costs:	
Payments for days not worked	Paid holidays and compensation for holidays not taken – holiday bonuses – public holidays and other paid holidays – severance pay and payments in lieu of notice
Social welfare costs	Contributions for social welfare and family allowances paid by the firm
Statutory social welfare costs	Health, maternity and disability insurance – retirement pension – unemployment insurance – guaranteed salary/wage in case of illness – occupational illness – industrial accident – family allowances – other
Customary, contractual or voluntary costs	Mutual insurance on a firm or industry basis – supplementary retirement and provident schemes – contractual or voluntary guaranteed wage/salary – supplementary redundancy insurance scheme – customary, contractual or voluntary family allowances and other family subsidies – other

Table 2.1 *continued*

Classification	*Content of the EC survey*
Benefits in kind	Payments in kind and corresponding compensatory payments – housing, housing allowances and payments to building schemes – Other payments in kind (coal, gas, electricity, food and drink, footwear, clothing, etc.) or corresponding compensatory payments – Special levies (taxes and dues)
Other expenses of social nature	Other social expenditure – miscellaneous liabilities (direct and indirect payments) – liabilities under the Disabled Persons Acts (FRG only) – special levies (taxes and dues)
Vocational training	Vocational training costs – vocational training costs excluding apprentices' wages – apprentices' wages – special levies (taxes and dues)
Taxes and subsidies	UK only: special employment tax and refunds thereof, and regional assistance (Selective Employment Tax up to April 1973 and Regional Employment Premiums). (The heading is negative if the premiums and refunds exceed taxes.)

particular types of cost within a broad range, there are advantages to be gained from increasing the detail.

The wage and non-wage classifications of the four countries inevitably differ considerably and an initial task is to devise a standard of comparison. The standard chosen is that adopted by the European Communities (EC) in their surveys of the structure of labour costs, which appear at triennial intervals. Two of the four countries, the UK and West Germany (FRG), reconstruct their own individual surveys to conform to the EC classification, while for Japan and the USA appropriate conversions have to be attempted. Full descriptions of data sources, survey methods, individual country labour cost categories and conversions to the EC standard are given in Appendix Tables A2.1–A2.6.

The nine major cost categories under the EC classification are divided into two parts – wage costs and non-wage costs – as follows:

Wage costs	*Non-wage costs*
Direct remuneration and regular bonuses	Payment for days not worked
Payments to workers' savings schemes	Social welfare costs – statutory social welfare costs – customary, contractual and voluntary costs
Other bonuses and gratuities	Benefits in kind Other expenses of a social nature Vocational training costs Taxes and subsidies

A breakdown of the cost items within each of these categories is presented in Table 2.1.

At least three shortcomings arise with this classification. First, given the way the data are recorded in each country, it is impossible in practice to achieve a rigid distinction between wage and non-wage costs. A major problem concerns the category 'payments for days not worked'. For example, overtime work undertaken on statutory holidays often entails overtime bonus payments *and* holidays in lieu of those worked. In this classification, the former enters under wage costs while the latter is treated as a non-wage and yet, conceptually, the distinction is difficult to make. Indeed, in some countries, large components of payments for days not worked may be argued to be direct remuneration since labour contracts often relate holiday entitlements to the length and type of work performed. In the FRG, for example, workers are entitled to holiday pay, over an agreed period, based on average earnings over the thirteen weeks immediately before the holiday. However, since it is possible to separate the 'payment for days not worked' items from the other labour cost categories, definitional difficulties are substantially minimised.

Secondly, there seems to be little doubt that, for some categories of cost, the published figures significantly underestimate the expenditure involved. By far the greatest problem in this respect concerns the category 'vocational training'. It is clearly extremely difficult, and probably prohibitively expensive, for major national surveys to measure training costs adequately. A full appraisal would involve estimating the rental value of physical training facilities, the cost of instruction, the cost of replacing workers involved in recurrent training programmes, and so on. It is doubtful, also, whether the voluntary social welfare payments under the item 'social welfare costs' fully represent all such non-statutory undertakings by the firm. It is likely, therefore, that statutory payments may well have too high a weight and firms' voluntary contributions too low a weight, given the former's more comprehensive and systematic administrative control and measurement.

Thirdly, as can be seen in the Appendix Tables A 2.2–A 2.5, there is quite a wide variation in the range and coverage within each cost category in the four countries. In general, West Germany and Japan present the most detailed information.[1]

2.2 ENDOGENOUS AND EXOGENOUS COSTS

In Table 2.1, social welfare payments are divided into two subcategories: those that are statutorily imposed on firms and those undertaken by firms following collective bargaining agreements or voluntary commitments. This latter type of cost introduces an important choice, or endogenous element into the firm's NWLC structure.

Table 2.2 *Endogenous and exogenous non-wage labour costs:[a] UK and US manufacturing industries, 1973–81*

		As proportion of total labour costs	
Category of NWLC	*Year*	*UK*	*USA*
Endogenous[b]	1972/3[d]	6.8	9.4
	1975	8.0	10.1
	1978	9.9	10.6
	1981	9.8	10.8
Exogenous[c]	1972/3[d]	5.4	6.5
	1975	6.9	6.8
	1978	8.8	7.5
	1981	9.5	7.8
Ratio (endogenous/exogenous)	1972/3[d]	1.3	1.5
	1975	1.2	1.5
	1978	1.1	1.4
	1981	1.0	1.4

[a] Holiday payments are excluded from these estimates.
[b] Includes voluntary social welfare costs, benefits in kind, other expenses of a social nature, vocational training.
[c] Statutory social welfare costs.
[d] USA figures refer to 1972 and UK figures to 1973.
Sources: see Table A2.1.

Other similar expenditures include benefits in kind, holiday payments above statutorily legislated norms,[2] and most elements of training costs. Much of the existing NWLC literature has been concerned with the exogenous elements of the costs, or at least has treated the costs as if they were exogenous, and it will be useful to later developments to emphasise the distinction. In order to gain an impression of the relative importance of the endogenous element of the costs, Table 2.2 presents estimates of endogenous and exogenous costs as proportions of total labour costs in the UK and USA for the years 1973, 1975, 1978 and 1981. While the relative importance of endogenous NWLCs is strongly suggested in Table 2.2 (given ratios of endogenous to exogenous NWLCs in excess of unity), the figures presented probably overestimate their relative weight. This occurs because payments for days not worked are omitted from the calculations. Such payments contain endogenous and exogenous elements that are impossible to separate adequately. Statutory holidays are clearly exogenous while other holidays are determined in part by minimum standards set by legislation. Some holiday entitlements, on the other hand, may well involve a wide discretion over payment and length. Despite their importance, however, there is some indication in Table 2.2 of a gradual decline in the proportion of endogenous to exogenous costs over the past decade.

It is not possible with our data to disaggregate further those elements of the endogenous NWLCs that are voluntarily[3] undertaken by firms and those that arise out of collective bargaining. Some information on voluntary payments can be obtained, however, at a more micro level. For example, a breakdown of the total labour costs of the large German chemical firm, Bayer, for the years 1976–80 is shown in Table 2.3. Typical of capital-intensive industries (see Chapter 3),

Table 2.3 *Wages and non-wages as a percentage of total labour costs: Bayer AG (FRG), 1976–80*

Labour costs	*1976*	*1977*	*1978*	*1979*	*1980*
Wages and salaries	49.2	49.2	50.9	47.2	48.6
Statutory and contractual NWLCs	27.7	29.7	29.4	28.0	29.4
Voluntary NWLCs	23.1	21.1	19.7	24.8	22.0
Total	100.0	100.0	100.0	100.0	100.0

Source: G. Broja, 'Personalnebenleistungen in der betrieblichen Bewährung – Beispiele aus der Bayer AG', in *Analytic '81, 3. Symposium der Consulectra*, Hamburg, 23–24 November 1981.

the firm has proportionately high non-wages, which are in excess of 50 per cent of total labour costs. Of these, about 40 per cent are purely voluntary payments undertaken by the firm. Again this latter percentage is probably atypical since the firm's relatively highly skilled labour force undoubtedly accounts for a higher than average voluntary commitment (see Chapter 4). However, the figures indicate that, in general, such costs are likely to be a significant proportion of total NWLCs.

Table 2.4 gives an indication of the various categories of voluntary payments as well as the relative cost importance of each category for industries in the Ruhr–Niederrhein area of the FRG. An interesting feature is that training costs, like voluntary old age pension payments, grew substantially between 1964 and 1980 and yet still make up less than 20 per cent of the total voluntary payments. If we assume that voluntary payments are 25 per cent of total labour costs, almost certainly an overestimate of their average weight, then training costs would account for less than 5 per cent of total labour costs. This crude estimate is higher than indicated by our main data sources (see Chapter 3), but nevertheless represents a proportion that is significantly smaller than some other NWLC categories. Apart from problems of measurement, another complication arises when assessing the relative importance of training costs. Unlike the other payments in Table 2.4, training costs are highly related to labour turnover, given that they particularly concern new hires. Also, changes in technology and work organisation influence the degree to which retraining is required. Thus, for example, a given training-cost proportion might

Table 2.4 *Structure of voluntary non-wage labour costs in Rhein–Ruhr Employers' Federation (FRG)*

Item	*1964* %	*1980* %
Old age pension	20.7	28.4
Allowances	42.4	24.5
Vocational training	10.1	18.8
Canteens	4.1	6.8
Social facilities	1.2	3.8
Health	3.6	3.6
Security services	1.0	2.8
Clothes	0.9	2.6
Others	16.0	8.7
Total	100.0	100.0

Source: *Handelsblatt,* (Düsseldorf) 11 – 12 March 1981.

appear to be relatively low compared to other proportions when in fact it may constitute a highly significant once-over cost if labour turnover itself is relatively low.

Most subsequent references to the category 'customary, contractual or voluntary costs' in Table 2.1 will be made under the somewhat simpler heading 'non-obligatory costs'.

2.3 QUASI-FIXED AND VARIABLE COSTS

While the implications of the distinction between endogenous and exogenous costs have not been fully explored in the economics literature, a great emphasis has been laid on a different NWLC dichotomy. This concerns the fact that a proportion of the costs are *per-worker* costs while the remainder are *per-manhour* costs. These are usually referred to, respectively, as quasi-fixed and variable NWLCs. (Since the main concerns of this text are with short-run phenomena, the word 'fixed' will be used interchangeably with 'quasi-fixed'.) The classic example of a fixed cost is training expenditure. In general, a certain sum is invested in training (or retraining) a worker irrespective of the subsequent hours worked utilising the acquired skill. Statutory social welfare payments, on the other hand, are usually related strictly to earnings per worker and, therefore, hours of work. For several of our NWLC items, the division between fixed and variable elements is fairly simple to make. However, statutory social welfare contributions can provide complications. These will be discussed before attempting some estimates of the relative importance of the fixed costs.

In all four of the countries, as well as most other countries in the OECD bloc, the basic method by which firms contribute to statutory social welfare schemes is the same. Contributions are made to each main item of social welfare – for example old age pensions and sickness cover – in the form of a payroll tax up to some specified ceiling limit. For workers with earnings below a given ceiling, the tax constitutes a variable, earnings-related NWLC; providing the ceiling is not crossed, increased earnings necessitate increased contributions. For workers with earnings above the ceiling, the tax takes the form of a fixed per capita NWLC; an increase in earnings, through more overtime for instance, will not lead to a higher level of contribution. Changes in per capita contributions per period of time, therefore, can occur through changes in the payroll tax rates and/or changes in the ceiling limits. Details concerning the composition of the statutory social welfare system in the four countries as well as the various tax rates and ceiling limits are shown in Appendix Tables A2.7 and A2.8.

Table 2.5 *Ratio of statutory social security ceilings to average wages, 1975 – 9*

Year	Japan				UK	USA				FRG			
	1	2	3[a]	4[b]	1 – 4[c]	1	2	3	4[a]	1	2	3	4
1975	1.16	1.16	—	—	1.34	1.38	1.38	0.41	—	1.50	1.12	1.50	1.61
1977	1.67	1.67	—	—	1.67	1.40	1.40	0.38	—	1.58	1.19	1.58	n.a.
1979	1.76	1.76	—	—	1.63	1.78	1.78	0.47	—	1.68	1.26	1.68	1.26

1 = old age pension.
2 = sickness benefit.
3 = unemployment benefit.
4 = industrial injury.

[a] No ceiling limit.
[b] Not applicable.
[c] One tax rate and ceiling limit applies to all social welfare payments.

Sources: 'Comparative Tables of the Social Security Systems', in *Member States of the European Communities* (Paris: EEC, 1981); *National Accounts, 1963 – 1980* (Paris: OECD, 1982); US Dept. of Health and Human Resources, *Social Security Programs throughout the World* (Washington, DC: US Government Printing Office, 1979).

The pertinent information for present purposes is given in Table 2.5, which shows the ratios of ceilings to wages for the four main types of social security payment. A ratio equal to 1 represents a ceiling limit equal to the average wage. As the ratio tends to zero, then all contributions become fixed labour costs.

Apart from unemployment insurance payments in the USA and, to a much lesser extent, sickness contributions in the FRG, the ratios in Table 2.5 are relatively high. In these cases, firms' contributions predominantly take the form of variable labour costs. Allocating the exact proportions of the workforce that lie above and below the ceiling necessitates a detailed earnings distribution for each period of time. While this is not possible to achieve generally, the distribution in relation to the ceiling can be worked out quite accurately for the UK in 1978 (see Table 2.6). The actual ceiling limit was set at £120 per week in that year and it can be seen that, apart from non-manual male workers (with 23 per cent above the ceiling), all other groups exhibit very low above-ceiling percentage rates. Note that, in order to achieve a UK ceiling/wage ratio equivalent to the USA unemployment insurance ratios in Table 2.5, the ceiling would have to be set at £30–£60 for men and less than £30 for women, in which case the social welfare payments would overwhelmingly represent fixed labour costs.

From the last row in Table 2.6, it is clear that disaggregating wage groups by sex and skill produces a wide variation in the ceiling/wage

Table 2.6 *Percentage of UK manual and non-manual employees above actual*[a] *and notional contribution ceilings, 1978*

Earnings above £	*Full-time men aged 21 +*			*Full-time women aged 21 +*		
	Manual	*Non-Manual*	*All*	*Manual*	*Non-Manual*	*All*
30	99.8	99.7	99.8	95.0	97.4	96.8
60	80.6	88.2	83.8	18.8	38.0	32.7
80	44.6	65.3	53.2	3.0	15.4	11.9
100	18.0	40.4	27.4	0.7	5.3	4.0
110	11.2	31.3	19.6	0.3	3.3	2.4
120	6.8	23.1	13.6	0.2	1.7	1.3
150	1.7	10.1	5.2	0	0.3	0.3
200	0.3	3.2	1.5	0	0.1	0.1
250	0.1	1.2	0.6	0	0	0
Average weekly earnings (£)	78.4	99.9	86.9	48.0	58.5	55.6
Actual ceiling/ earnings ratio	1.5	1.2	1.4	2.5	2.1	2.2

[a] Actual ceiling = £120 per week

Source: Calculated from the earnings distributions given in the *Department of Employment Gazette* (London: HMSO, October 1978, p. 1142).

ratios. This is illustrated further in Table 2.7, where the main FRG statutory contribution ratios are broken down in the same way. It is evident that in the case of the largest statutory surcharge, health insurance, there is a large fixity element involved in contributions for white-collar male workers. This suggests wide variations in the degree of fixed social welfare costs across industries, with high fixity proportions occurring in highly skilled, male-dominated industries[4] where, of course, average wages are highest.

With this background in mind, Table 2.8 presents estimates of the ratio of fixed to variable labour costs for the UK and USA. Excluding holiday payments and US unemployment insurance (UI) contributions (see below), all NWLCs apart from statutory social welfare payments are treated as fixed labour costs. Given the high ceiling/wage ratios shown in Table 2.6, all the UK statutory contributions have been allocated to variable costs. In the USA, on the other hand, all payments under the OASDHI (old age, survivor, disability and health insurance) system (items 1, 2 and 4 in Table 2.5) are treated as variable costs, while the unemployment insurance contributions, with very low ceilings, are treated as being purely fixed. This latter allocation ignores

Table 2.7 *Ratios of ceilings to average wages by sex and occupation: FRG, 1975–80*

Year	Skill group	Old age pension			Health insurance			Unemployment insurance		
		Male	Female	Both	Male	Female	Both	Male	Female	Both
1975	A	1.50	2.24	1.61	1.12	1.67	1.21	1.50	2.24	1.61
	B	1.13	1.78	1.32	0.85	1.33	0.90	1.13	1.78	1.32
1977	A	1.56	2.29	1.67	1.17	1.72	1.25	1.56	2.29	1.67
	B	1.21	1.41	1.40	0.90	1.41	1.05	1.21	1.41	1.40
1979	A	1.64	2.40	1.75	1.23	1.80	1.31	1.64	2.40	1.75
	B	1.26	1.95	1.55	0.94	1.46	1.09	1.26	1.95	1.55
1980	A	1.63	2.38	1.73	1.22	1.78	1.30	1.63	2.38	1.73
	B	1.23	1.91	1.42	0.92	1.55	1.06	1.23	1.91	1.42

A = blue-collar workers.
B = white-collar workers.

Sources: Statistisches Bundesamt Wiesbaden, Fachserie 16, *Löhne und Gehälter*, Reihe 2.1 'Arbeiterverdienste in der Industrie'; Reihe 2.2 'Angestelltenverdienste in der Industrie' (Stuttgart/Mainz: 1975, 1977, 1979, 1980); and 'Comparative Tables of the Social Security Systems', in *National Accounts, 1963–1980* (Paris: OECD, 1982).

Table 2.8 *Estimates of fixed and variable labour costs: UK and US manufacturing industries, 1973–8*

Type of labour cost[a]	UK				USA			
	1973	1975	1978	1981	1973	1975	1978	1981
Fixed NWLC I [b]	6.59	7.84	9.60	9.60	10.27	10.83	11.62	10.76
Fixed NWLC II[c]	14.38	16.98	18.20	20.50	19.00	20.09	20.50	19.68
Variable NWLC	5.40	6.80	8.80	9.40	5.64	6.06	6.25	7.95
Variable LC	80.85	77.21	73.30	70.70	75.36	73.85	73.05	72.37
Total variable LC	86.25	84.01	82.10	80.10	81.00	79.91	79.29	80.32
Ratio I (fixed/variable)[b]	0.08	0.09	0.12	0.12	0.13	0.14	0.15	0.13
Ratio II (fixed/variable)[c]	0.17	0.20	0.22	0.26	0.23	0.25	0.26	0.25

[a] The figures in the first five rows are expressed as a percentage of total labour costs.
[b] Excluding payments for days not worked.
[c] Including payments for days not worked.

Sources: see Table A2.1.

Table 2.9 *Fixed/variable cost ratios, overtime and skill ratios: UK manufacturing industry, 1978*

Industry	*Ratio I*	*Rank (1)*	*Ratio II*	*Rank (2)*	*Weekly overtime hours per worker*	*Rank (3)*	*Ratio of non-manual to total workers*	*Rank (4)*
Production and preliminary processing of metals	0.14	2	0.26	2	3.59	2	0.28	6
Manufacture of non-metallic mineral products	0.10	9	0.20	9	3.56	3	0.24	11
Chemical industry	0.17	1	0.28	1	3.16	6	0.44	1
Man-made fibres industry	0.13	3	0.23	4	3.86	1	0.27	7
Manufacture of metal products	0.11	6	0.21	8	2.58	9	0.25	9
Mechanical engineering	0.12	5	0.23	4	3.34	4	0.35	5
Electrical engineering	0.11	6	0.22	6	2.08	12	0.37	3
Instrument engineering	0.13	3	0.24	3	2.09	11	0.42	2
Textile industry	0.06	13	0.16	13	1.75	13	0.19	13
Leather and leather goods industry	0.06	13	0.15	14	1.38	14	0.18	14
Manufacture of clothing and footwear	0.06	13	0.15	14	0.37	15	0.17	15
Timber and wooden furniture industries	0.10	9	0.17	12	2.60	7	0.23	12
Manufacture of paper and paper products, printing and publishing	0.11	6	0.22	6	3.22	5	0.36	4
Processing of rubber and plastics	0.10	9	0.20	9	2.60	7	0.26	8
Other manufacturing industries	0.10	9	0.19	11	2.18	10	0.25	9
Spearman's rank coefficients (R^S)	$R^S_{13} = 0.66$		$R^S_{14} = 0.87$		$R^S_{23} = 0.64$		$R^S_{24} = 0.91$	

Sources: *Eurostat:* see Table A2.1; *Department of Employment Gazette* (London: HMSO).

a further complication in the US system. (In fact, there are several US unemployment insurance systems; for interesting discussions of the predominant one, the so-called reserve ratio method, see Brechling, 1977; Topel and Welch, 1980.) In the event of an employee changing employers in a given tax year, the unemployment insurance tax is non-transferable. This means that if turnover in a given job is such that two, three or more employees hold the job within the tax year then the *full* taxable base (currently standing at US $6,000) will apply two, three or more times. In general, therefore, the higher the turnover rate, the greater the number of jobs with contributions related to average earnings since the higher is the *effective* tax ceiling. However, in a macro context, the quantitative importance of rapid turnover in the USA has been strongly questioned in recent years (see, for example, Akerlof, 1979; Hall, 1982), and so this variable element in the costs is discounted here. The resulting upward fixity bias in allocating all UI contributions and all private social welfare payments (see Ehrenberg and Schumann, 1982[5]) to fixed costs will cancel out, to some extent, with the equivalent downward fixity bias in allocating all OASDHI payments to variable costs.

As mentioned earlier, there is some ambiguity concerning the degree to which the cost item 'payments for days not worked' is independent of direct labour costs. To the extent to which it constitutes an NWLC, then it is primarily a fixed cost. Ratios I and II in Table 2.8 are calculated, respectively, with and without this item included. There is little doubt, however, that Ratio II represents the more reasonable estimate, putting fixed labour costs at roughly 20 per cent of total variable costs in both countries. By both methods, the ratio estimates for the UK and the USA are reasonably similar: both countries exhibit approximately the same sized ratios and both show a relatively modest ratio growth for the period 1973–78. After 1978, the US ratios decline somewhat, unlike their UK counterparts. These aggregate data, however, disguise a wide inter-industry variation in the ratios. The UK ratios are broken down at two-digit manufacturing industry level in Table 2.9 and show a range for Ratios I and II of 0.06–0.17 and 0.15–0.28, respectively. These and the other data in this table are referred to further at later stages.

APPENDIX

Data on Non-Wage Labour Costs in FRG, Japan, UK and USA

Table A2.1 *Survey methods, definitions and sources of non-wage labour costs*

	Japan	*UK*	*USA*	*FRG*
Survey methods	Conducted through field interviews by each prefectural Labour Standards Bureau, Labour Standards Inspection Office and enumerators	National questionnaire based on the EC framework	Questionnaire conducted by the Chamber of Commerce of the United States	National questionnaire based on the EC framework
Number of establishments covered by the survey	6,000 enterprises with 30 + employees, all industries and services	Firms in all industries with 50 + employees in 1972 and 10 + employees thereafter: 1972: 19,000 firms 1975: 71,118 firms 1978: not available 1981: not available	All industries (of which manufacturing) 1973: 742 (437) 1975: 761 (445) 1978: 858 (497) 1981: not available	Firms with 10 + employees, all industries 1972: 99,678 (50 + = 28,767) 1975: 91,963 1978: not available 1981: not available
Number of employees covered by the survey	not available	1972: 6,962,000 1975: 7,091,000 1978: 8,189,000 1981: 7,389,000	Not available	1972: 9,737,000 (50 + = 8,258,000) 1975: 8,397,000 1978: 8,700,000 1981: 8,505,000
Type of employee covered	Only *regular* employees	*Manual workers* are those engaged in manual work in the establishment, even if they are paid on a monthly basis.	In general, limited to employees who are not exempt from the Fair Labor Standards Act	As in the UK

		comprise all other employees, including foremen, supervisory staff, engineers, management executives and managerial staff. *Excluded* are home workers and cleaners working only a few hours a week. *Treated separately* are apprentices and trainees		
Time-units of costs	Average monthly labour costs per regular employee	Average hourly cost per manual employee and average monthly cost per non-manual Average hourly costs per manual and non-manual combined	Average annual cost per employee	As in the UK
Classification	As near as possible to EC classification	EC classification	As near as possible to EC classification	EC classification
Source	'Survey of Welfare Facilities System for Employees', *Year Book of Labour Statistics* (Tokyo: Ministry of Labour, Statistics and Information Department, 1975, 1978, 1981); plus unpublished statistical material.	'Labour Costs in Industry', *Eurostat* (Luxembourg: Statistical Office of the European Communities, 1966, 1969, 1972, 1975, 1977, and unpublished latest figures)	US Chamber of Commerce, *Employee Benefits* (Washington, DC: US Chamber Survey Research Center, 1966, 1969, 1973, 1975, 1978, 1981)	'Labour Costs in Industry', *Eurostat* (Luxembourg: Statistical Office of the European Communities, 1966,1969, 1972, 1975, 1977, and unpublished latest figures)

Table A2.2 *Labour cost categories: FRG*

(1) Direct remuneration
(2) Special payments
gratuities, special '13th' annual payment (*Weihnachtsgeld*), profit-sharing, holiday bonuses, payments to workers' savings schemes
(3) Payments for days not worked
holiday payments, sickness payments, guaranteed sick pay, payment for statutory holidays and other days off
(4) Contributions to social security
compulsory employers' payments to social security insurance, retirement, sickness and unemployment insurance, industrial accident, other expenses including payments to industrial retirement pension and net payments to private pension funds
(5) Other non-wage labour costs
layoff payments (or severance pay), other payments by law (seriously disabled persons, maternity, etc), family allowances, lodging allowances, support in the case of illness, food allowances, benefits in kind, expenses of social nature (canteens, facilities, etc.), vocational training, apprentices' wages, other allowances

Source: Statistisches Bundesamt Wiesbaden (ed.), Fachserie 16, *Löhne und Gehälter*, 'Personal- und Personalnebenkosten', Heft 1: 'Aufwendungen der Arbeitgeber im Produzierenden Gewerbe' (Stuttgart/Mainz).

Table A2.3 *Labour cost categories: UK*

(1) Wages and salaries
(2) Bonuses
(3) Holidays, other time off with pay, and sickness
(4) Statutory national insurance contributions
(5) Provisions for redundancy
(6) Employee liability insurance
(7) Voluntary social welfare

superannuation and pension funds
provision for sickness and industrial accidents
lump sum and *ex gratia* payments

(8) Benefits in kind
(9) Subsidised services
(10) Training
(11) Government subsidies (negative cost)

Source: *Department of Employment Gazette* (London, HMSO), September 1980.

Table A2.4 *Labour cost categories: Japan*

(1) Total cash earnings[a]
regular wages (including family allowances, housing allowance, community allowance, rest-day allowance), overtime allowance, bonus, others
(2) Cost of severance pay
(3) Cost of payments in kind
(4) Social security costs
cost of obligatory social welfare services (health insurance, welfare pension, labour insurance, including workers' accident compensation and employment insurance, others, including children's allowance, coal mining pension, employment benefit for handicapped), cost of non-obligatory welfare services (including company housing, medical and health services, canteens and other food services, cultural, sporting and recreational facilities, private insurance plans, supplementary workmen's accident compensation, solatium for congratulations and condolences)
(5) Cost of education
(6) Cost of recruitment
(7) Other labour costs

[a] The Japanese statistics do not classify the item 'payment for days not worked'. It is implicitly included in cash earnings. For method of estimation, see Table A2.6.

Source: see Table A2.1.

Table A2.5 *Labour cost categories: USA*

(1) Total payroll dollars

(2) Legally required payments

old-age, survivors, disability and health insurance (FICA taxes) unemployment compensation, workers' compensation (including estimated cost of self-insured), railroad retirement tax, railroad unemployment and cash sickness insurance, state sickness benefits insurance, etc.

(3) Pension, insurance and other agreed-upon payments

pension plan premiums and pension payments not covered by insurance-type plan (net), life insurance premiums, death benefits, hospital, surgical, medical and major medical insurance premiums, etc. (net), salary continuation or long-term disability, dental insurance premiums, discounts on goods and services purchased from company by employees, employees' meals furnished by company, compensation payments in excess of legal requirements, separation or termination pay allowances, moving expenses, etc.

(4) Paid rest periods, lunch periods, wash-up time, travel time, clothes change time, get-ready time, etc.

(5) Payments for time not worked

paid vactions and payments in lieu of vacation, payments for holidays not worked, paid sick leave, payments for State or National Guard duty, jury, witness and voting pay allowances, payments for time lost due to death in family or other personal reasons, etc.

(6) Other items

profit-sharing payments, contributions to employee thrift plans, Christmas or other special bonuses, service awards, suggestion awards, etc., employee education expenditures (tuition refunds, etc.), special wage payments ordered by courts, payments to union stewards, etc.

Source: see Table A2.1

Table A2.6 *Re-classification of Japanese and US non-wage labour costs by EC method*

EC classification	*Japanese equivalent*	*US equivalent*
Direct remuneration and regular bonuses Other bonuses and gratuities Savings	Total cash earnings – (family allowance + housing allowance + community allowance + rest-day allowance + bonus + 'others' + payments for days not worked)	Total payroll dollars
Payments for days not worked	Calculation (monthly figure):[a] (Monthly regular wages)/(Average monthly working hours) × 8 hours × (days of paid leave and paid holidays actually taken) $\times \frac{1}{12}$	Paid rest periods Paid vacations and payments in lieu of vacation Payments for holidays not worked Payments for State or National Guard duty, jury, witness and voting pay allowances; payments for time lost due to death in family or other personal reasons, etc.
Statutory social welfare costs	Health insurance contribution Welfare pension contribution Labour insurance contribution Others	Old age, survivors, disability and health insurance (FICA taxes) Unemployment compensation (including estimated cost of self-insured) Railroad retirement tax Railroad unemployment and cash sickness insurance State sickness benefits insurance, etc. Paid sick leave[e]

continued

Table A2.6 *continued*

EC classification	*Japanese equivalent*	*US equivalent*
Customary, contractual or voluntary social welfare costs	Cost of medical and health services Contribution to private insurance plans Cost of supplementary workmen's accident compensation Cost of solatium for congratulations and condolences Family allowances[b] Cost of severance pay	Pension plan premiums and pension payments not covered by insurance-type plan (net) Life insurance premiums, death benefits, hospital, surgical, medical and major medical insurance premiums etc. (net), short-term disability Salary continuation or long-term disability Dental insurance premiums Contributions to privately financed unemployment benefit funds, separation or termination pay allowances
Benefits in kind	Cost of canteens and other food services[c] Cost of payments in kind Housing allowances[b] Cost of company housing[c]	Discounts on goods and services purchased from company by employees[f] Employees' meals furnished by company[f]
Other expenses of social nature	Cost of cultural, sporting and recreational facilities[c] Other costs of non-obligatory welfare services[c] Community allowances[b] Other labour costs	Miscellaneous payments (compensation payments in excess of legal requirements, separation or termination pay allowances, moving expenses, etc.) Profit-sharing payments Contributions to employee thrift plans

Table A2.6 *continued*

EC classification	*Japanese equivalent*	*US equivalent*
		Christmas or other special bonuses; service awards, suggestion awards etc. Special wage payments ordered by courts, payments to union stewards, etc.
Vocational training	Cost of education and vocational training Cost of recruitment[d]	Employee education expenditure (tuition refunds, etc.)
Taxes and subsidies	—	—

[a] There is no Japanese item 'payments for days not worked'. Such payments are included in cash earnings. Special tables were obtained that showed:

(i) the days of paid leave and paid holidays that were actually taken by employees and
(ii) a breakdown of the content of total cash earnings.

Monthly estimates of 'payments for days not worked' were then calculated as shown.

[b] Taken from 'cash earnings'.
[c] Taken from 'non-obligatory welfare costs'.
[d] Costs of recruitment (not available for countries other than Japan) has been included as part of vocational training.
[e] Taken from 'payments for days not worked'.
[f] Taken from 'voluntary social welfare costs'.

Table A2.7 *Social welfare definitions*

Eurostat classifies social security contributions and family allowances paid by the employer under the headings:

Statutory contributions
- sickness, maternity, disablement, retirement and unemployment insurance;
- guaranteed sick pay;
- insurance against industrial accidents and occupational diseases;
- family allowances;
- others.

Customary, contractual or voluntary payments
- insurance taken out by the firm or branch;
- supplementary retirement insurance scheme;
- contractual or voluntary guaranteed sick or accident pay (supplementary pay);
- supplementary unemployment insurance;
- contractual additional family benefits and other family allowances;
- others.

1 Japan

There are many types of social insurance cover in Japan, although the largest in scale and the most important are the Health Insurance, National Health Insurance, Employees' Pension Insurance and National Pension. The system covers the following range of items:

Employment insurance
- job applicant benefits
- basic allowance for general employees
- skill acquisition allowance
- boarding allowance
- sickness and injury allowance
- benefits for the insured in special short-term employment and the insured day labourers
- employment promotion benefits
- outfit and allowance for full-time employment
- moving expenses
- wider-area job-seeking expenses

Health insurance
- cash benefits in the case of diseases, injuries, childbirth, death.

Pension insurance
- old age pension
- survivors' pension

Table A2.7 *continued*

- withdrawal grant
- workmen's accident compensation insurance
- children's allowance

2 UK

The state social security system is highly integrated. Each employer and employee pays a contribution into a national fund, which provides the social benefits. The main items are:

- retirement pension
- sickness benefit
- invalidity benefit
- maternity allowance
- unemployment benefit
- widow's allowance
- death grant

3 US social security system

The main parts of the American statutory social security system are:

OASDHI
- old age
- survivor
- disability
- hospital insurance

Unemployment compensation

Railroad workers have a separate social insurance system of their own.

4 FRG

Unemployment insurance
The present social security system provides the following benefits:

- unemployment benefits
- measures for job security
- bad weather pay
- short-time subsidy
- special measures for creating employment

continued

Table A2.7 *continued*

Statutory sickness insurance
- measures for preventing sickness
- rehabilitation benefits
- medical care
- maternity allowances
- death grant
- family allowances

Retirement insurance
- disability benefits and accident insurances
- retirement pensions
- survivors' benefits

Sources:
1 Die soziale Sicherheit in den Ländern der EG', in *Die Ortskrankenkasse* (Bonn), 9 October 1979.
2 D. Callund, *Employee Benefits in Europe, An International Survey of State and Private Schemes in 16 Countries* (New York, NY: Gower, 1975).
3 *Which Benefits?* Leaflet FB. 2 (London: Department of Health and Social Security, November 1980).
4 'Comparative Tables of the Social Security Systems', in *Member States of the European Communities* (Paris: EEC, 1981).
5 Japanese Industrial Relations Series, Vol. 5, *Social Security* (Tokyo: The Japanese Institute of Labour, 1980).

Table A2.8 *Social welfare tax rates and ceiling limits (monthly) – employers' share only*

Country	*1975* % *rate*	*1975* *Ceiling*	*1976* % *rate*	*1976* *Ceiling*		*1977* % *rate*	*1977* *Ceiling*	*1978* % *rate*	*1978* *Ceiling*	*1979* % *rate*	*1979* *Ceiling*
Japan:											
1 [a]	3.80	Yen 200,000	4.55	≤7/76 [f]	Yen 200,000	4.55	Yen 320,000	4.55	Yen 320,000	4.55	Yen 320,000
				>8/76	Yen 320,000						
2	3.80	Yen 200,000	3.90	≤6/76	Yen 200,000	3.90	Yen 320,000	3.90	Yen 380,000	4.00	Yen 380,000
				>7/76	Yen 320,000						
3	0.80	—	0.80		—	0.80	—	0.80	—	0.90	—
UK:											
1 – 4 [b]	8.50	£299	8.75	£411.67		10.75	£455	12.0	£520	13.5	£585
USA:											
1	4.95 }	$14,100 (yr)	4.95 }	$15,300 (yr)		4.95 }	$16,500(yr)	5.05 }	$17,700 (yr)	5.08 }	$22,900 (yr)
2 [c]	0.90 }		0.90 }			0.90 }		1.00 }		1.05 }	
3 [d]	0.50	$ 4,200 (yr)	0.70	$ 4,200 (yr)		0.50	$ 4,200 (yr)	0.50	$ 6,000 (yr)	0.50	$ 6,000 (yr)
4 [d]	1.10	—	n.a.	—		1.30	—	n.a.	—	1.30	—
FRG:											
1	9.00	DM 2,800	9.00	DM 3,100		9.00	DM 3,400	9.00	DM 3,700	9.00	DM 4,000
2	5.25	DM 2,100	5.65	DM 2,325		5.70	DM 2,550	5.70	DM 2,775	5.60	DM 3,000
3	1.00	DM 2,800	1.50	DM 3,100		1.50	DM 3,400	1.50	DM 3,700	1.50	DM 4,000
4 [e]											

1 = old age, invalidity, death.
2 = sickness and maternity.
3 = unemployment.
4 = work injury.

[a] Welfare pension insurance.
[b] One general social welfare tax.
[c] Hospitalisation.
[d] Federal tax.

[e] Rate varies among the various professional organisations.
[f] ≤7/76 = up to and including July 1976.

Sources: 'Comparative Tables of the Social Security Systems' in *Member States of the European Communities* (Paris: EEC, 1981); *Social Security Programs throughout the World* (Washington, DC: US Dept. of Health, Education and Welfare, 1979); *Annual Abstract of Statistics*, 1981 edition, No. 117, (London: HMSO); *Annual Reports*, Tokyo: Council of the Social Security of the Office of Prime Minister.

NOTES

1 The prize for the most interesting NWLC item must go to Japan. Under voluntary social security costs is included 'cost of solatium for congratulations and condolences'; this can be obtained at two-digit industry level.

2 This includes not only statutory vacations, such as Christmas and New Year, but also other minimum holiday entitlements that are legislatively imposed. For example, the minimum annual holiday entitlement in the FRG, excluding public holidays, is eighteen days, whereas collective bargaining agreements can extend this to well over twenty days.

3 The word 'voluntary' is not intended to convey anything precise about the firm's motivation, and certainly should not be taken to be synonymous with any kind of philanthropic intent; it merely indicates a separation from statutorily imposed and collectively bargained non-wage payments. Some of the reasons for the firm incurring these costs are given in Chapters 4 and 10.

4 Some evidence of the fixed-cost – skill association, although in a broader context, is given in Table 2.9. The figures relate to the UK and high rank correlation coefficients are obtained between the ratio of fixed to total labour cost and the proportions of non-manual to total workers by manufacturing industry.

5 For reasons discussed in Chapter 9, Ehrenberg and Schumann (1982) also construct a fixed/variable labour cost ratio. They use three definitions of fixed costs, the second of which appears to be close to that adopted here. Their first measure is somewhat crude and need not concern us. Their third measure, however, adds firm contributions to private funds (health, welfare, vacation, etc.) as a variable cost. While, perhaps, the 'cancellation effect' mentioned in the text tips the balance in favour of the measure adopted here, it is not possible to discriminate accurately between the two estimates, both of which would be expected to give a reasonable degree of accuracy.

REFERENCES

Akerlof, G. A. (1979), 'The case against conservative macroeconomics', *Economica*, 46, 219–237.

Brechling, F. (1977), 'The incentive effects of the US unemployment insurance tax', *Research in Labor Economics,* Vol. 1, Greenwich, Conn.: JAI Press.

Ehrenberg, R. G. and P. L. Schumann (1982), *Longer Hours or More Jobs?* Cornell Studies in Industrial and Labor Relations No. 22, New York: Cornell University.

Hall, R. E. (1982), 'The importance of lifetime jobs in the US economy', *American Economic Review,* 72, 716–724.

Topel, R. and F. Welch (1980), 'Unemployment insurance; survey and extensions', *Economica,* 47, 301–322.

3 The Quantitative Importance of Non-Wage Labour Costs

On the basis of a fairly broad sample of OECD countries, Table 1.1 indicates that non-wage labour costs comprise 20–40 per cent of total labour costs. This chapter examines the degree to which each of the main cost categories shown in Table 2.1 contributes to these totals. It also investigates the changes in the absolute costs in real terms relative to real changes in productivity. As already indicated in Chapter 2, aggregate data on non-wages disguise a great complexity of variation among types of cost, occupational skill group and different industries. Here, these types of breakdown are studied in some more detail, concentrating on the four selected countries. As in Chapter 2, some of the distinctions made here will prove to be useful to later developments.

Table 3.1 disaggregates the ratios of NWLCs to total labour costs shown in Table 1.1 into the main constituent parts outlined in Table 2.1. It is immediately clear that a very high proportion of total NWLCs is made up of just two items. These are payments for days not worked and social welfare costs. In the UK, USA and FRG these items account for over 85 per cent of all NWLCs in 1978, while the comparable figure for Japan is 77 per cent. In 1978, the statutory and non-obligatory parts of social welfare contributions are of a reasonably similar magnitude in Japan, weighted somewhat towards statutory in the UK and somewhat towards non-obligatory in the USA. On the other hand, the FRG statutory contributions are 81 per cent of total social welfare costs. As can be seen in Table A2.8, FRG social welfare tax rates are significantly higher than in the other countries. Since FRG benefits are also, in general, higher, this might account for the fact that non-obligatory contributions are relatively low; higher statutory benefits may, to some extent, reduce both the demand for collectively agreed payments and the scope for unilateral employer initiatives.

In all countries, the single most significant influence on the growth of total NWLCs as a proportion of total labour costs has been the increase in social welfare contributions taken as a whole. Increases in both statutory and non-obligatory social welfare contributions have been significant in the UK and USA. As in the case of the levels of these ratios, the UK growth rates are weighted more towards statutory and

Table 3.1 *Non-wage labour costs as a proportion of total labour costs by type of cost: all industries, 1966–81*

Type of NWLC	*Year*	*Japan*[a]	*UK*[b]	*USA*	*FRG*[c]
Payments for days not worked	1966			7.8	9.5
	1969			8.1	
	1972		7.8	8.7	10.6
	1975	2.1	8.8	9.3	12.6
	1978	4.9	8.5	8.9	10.5
	1981		10.4	8.7	11.4
Total social welfare costs	1966			11.1	14.3
	1969			11.8	
	1972		9.5	13.9	16.8
	1975	11.1	11.7	14.9	17.6
	1978	12.9	15.1	16.0	20.3
	1981		15.7	16.7	19.9
Statutory social welfare	1966			5.3	11.3
	1969			5.7	
	1972		5.4	6.5	15.0
	1975	6.1	6.9	6.8	16.0
	1978	6.9	8.8	7.5	16.5
	1981		9.5	7.8	16.6
Customary, contractual or non-obligatory social welfare	1966			5.8	3.0
	1969			6.1	
	1972		4.1	7.4	1.8
	1975	5.0	4.8	8.1	1.6
	1978	6.1	6.3	8.5	3.8
	1981		6.2	8.9	3.3
Benefits in kind	1966			0.3	0.8
	1969			0.3	
	1972		0.4	0.3	0.4
	1975	3.1	0.3	0.3	0.4
	1978	3.3	0.4	0.2	0.2
	1981		0.4	0.2	0.2
Other expenses of social nature	1966			1.7	1.6
	1969			1.7	
	1972		1.3	1.6	0.9
	1975	1.4	1.1	1.6	0.8
	1978	1.7	1.4	1.8	0.7
	1981		1.2	1.5	0.8

Table 3.1 *continued*

Type of NWLC	*Year*	*Japan*[a]	*UK*[b]	*USA*	*FRG*[c]
Vocational training	1966			0.0[d]	1.0
	1969			0.1	
	1972		1.0	0.1	0.9
	1975	0.5	1.7	0.1	1.1
	1978	0.4	1.8	0.1	1.1
	1981		2.0	0.2	1.5
Taxes and subsidies	1966				
	1969				
	1972		-0.5		
	1975		-0.9		
	1978		-0.4		
	1981				
Total NWLC	1966			21.0	27.2
	1969			21.8	
	1972		19.4	24.6	29.6
	1975	18.3	22.9	26.1	32.9
	1978	23.2	26.8	27.0	32.8
	1981		29.7	27.3	33.8

[a] Japanese figures for 1966–72 are not available and, for 1981, key statistics to permit conversion to EC basis were not available at time of writing.
[b] UK 1966 figures are not shown since they are not recorded on a complete basis. There are no 1969 figures and the '1972' figures refer to 1973.
[c] There are no 1969 figures for FRG.
[d] US figures refer only to employee education expenditures (tuition refunds, etc.).

Sources: see Table A2.1.

the US more towards non-obligatory contributions. In the FRG, by contrast, practically the whole growth in the total social welfare cost ratio is due to statutory changes. In the USA, the non-obligatory cost ratio has grown consistently and significantly and the position is similar in the UK up to 1978, from which time it falls back slightly. A comparable growth rate is evident for Japan between the two available data points. In the FRG, however, the picture is quite different from the UK and USA, with a strong cyclical pattern in this ratio. Between 1966 and 1981, the US non-obligatory cost ratio has grown by 53 per cent, more than the comparable growth rate in the statutory cost ratio (47 per cent) and much more than the payment for days not worked ('payments') ratio (12 per cent). The UK non-obligatory cost ratio has grown almost the same amount (51 per cent) over the shorter period, 1973–81; this is less than the statutory cost ratio (76 per cent) but greater than the 'payments' ratio (33 per cent). The FRG, on the other hand, has experienced little overall growth in the non-obligatory cost ratio, which contrasts with growth rates of 47 and 20 per cent in the statutory cost and 'payments' ratios, respectively. At the end of the period, non-obligatory costs constitute 40–55 per cent of total social welfare costs in Japan, the UK and the USA. Again, in this latter respect, the FRG exhibits sharply contrasting figures, with statutory costs over four times greater than non-obligatory costs.

A notable feature of Table 3.1 is that it indicates that Japanese non-obligatory welfare payments are no bigger relative to wages than in the UK and USA; indeed, they are significantly smaller than in the latter country. This perhaps contrasts markedly with the image of the lifetime employment system in Japan whereby the firm provides employment security throughout the worker's occupational lifetime, coupled with a high degree of company benefits and facilities designed to improve each worker's occupational and leisure activities. It should be emphasised, however, that the lifetime employment system covers only 30–40 per cent of Japanese workers (see Cole, 1972; Patrick and Rosovsky, 1976) and tends to be concentrated in the larger companies. The resulting expectation that non-obligatory contributions should vary positively with firm size is supported by the evidence in Table 3.5. (This latter feature is also apparent in the FRG and UK, as suggested at a general level in Table 3.6 and in the case of private old age pensions in the FRG in Table 3.7). A further aspect of the Japanese labour market that probably serves to reduce the relative size of private social welfare is the fact that the compulsory age of retirement is between 55 and 60,[1] that is, five–ten years less than the retirement age in Europe. This would reduce the relative significance in Japan of deferred, seniority-based fringe benefits, which form an important part of non-obligatory payments in all four countries. It should be noted, however, that Japanese benefits in kind (e.g. canteen facilities, housing allowances – see Table A2.6) are significantly higher than in the other countries and this serves to redress the general social welfare balance somewhat.

As mentioned earlier, the relatively low proportions of vocational training costs to total costs[2] would be expected to disguise high inter-industry variation, given that these predominantly once-over costs are dependent on labour turnover as well as the sex- and skill-mix of the workforce. For example, in UK manufacturing industries in 1978, the ratio of training costs to total labour costs varies from 1.1 per cent in the textile and man-made fibres industries to 3.1 per cent in the mechanical engineering and timber industries.

Since 1972, the growth in the ratio of total NWLCs to total labour

Table 3.2 *Indices of real non-wage labour costs*[a] *and productivity*[b]*: UK, FRG and USA, manufacturing industry, 1972/3–1981 (1972/3 = 100)*

	UK				*FRG*				*USA*	
	NWLCs			*Productivity*	*NWLCs*			*Productivity*	*NWLCs*	*Productivity*
	Manual	*Non-manual*	*Total*		*Manual*	*Non-manual*	*Total*		*Total*	
1972 (FRG) 1973 (UK, US)	100	100	100	100	100	100	100	100	100	100
1975	140	122	131	99	132	125	131	113	105	99
1978	167	132	153	106	136	148	140	131	113	107
1981	202	156	185	112	154	157	155	144	108	110

[a] Average hourly costs (manual and total workers) and average monthly costs (non-manual workers) deflated by consumer price index.
[b] Output per person hour in 1972/3 prices.

Sources: *Eurostat*: see Table A2.1; *Department of Employment Gazette* (London: HMSO); Rolf Krengel *et al.*, *Produktionsvolumen und -potential*, 'Produktionsfaktoren des Bergbaus und des verarbeitenden Gerwerbes in der Bundesrepublik Deutschland' (Berlin: Deutsches Institut für Wirtschaftsforschung, 1972, 1975, 1978, 1981); Japanese *Year Book of Labour Statistics (International Section)*: see Table A2.1.

costs has been most marked in the UK (53 per cent) and weakest in the USA (11 per cent). Indeed, in the USA, there has been a distinct levelling off in the ratio in recent years. But, of course, while these ratios are a helpful way of illustrating the growing importance of NWLCs, a fuller appreciation of the costs' relative significance involves a wider set of relationships. It is obviously interesting, for example, to compare per-unit real increases in NWLCs and industrial productivity. A further insight would be gained by separating the cost and productivity increases by type of industry and, in particular, by capital and labour intensive industries. Some indication of these two additional considerations is given in Tables 3.2 and 3.3.

In Table 3.2, indices of real hourly (or monthly) NWLCs are compared to an index of real hourly productivity for the UK, FRG and USA for the period 1972/3–1981. Details of NWLCs are provided for manual and non-manual employees as well as the total workforce in the UK and FRG, while only total employee figures are available in the USA. The contrasts are stark. In the UK and FRG, average real NWLCs for all workers have risen by 85 and 55 per cent, respectively, over this period. This difference is due entirely to significantly higher cost increases for manual workers in the UK where real NWLCs actually doubled. When compared with productivity increases, however, the UK/FRG differences become much more exaggerated. The UK cost increases have occurred despite a mere 12 per cent improvement in hourly productivity; in other words, real NWLCs per unit of output have increased by 65 per cent over the period. In fact, between 1973 and 1975, a 31 per cent increase in costs accompanied a 1 per cent *fall* in productivity. While in the FRG, too, NWLC increases have outstripped productivity increases for both groups of workers in all years, the far more impressive productivity performance (44 per cent increase over the entire period) has resulted in a much lower increase in costs per unit of output (8 per cent increase over the entire period). The USA, with a productivity growth performance very similar to the UK, has managed, unlike the other two countries, to keep its costs per unit of output quite stable.[3] As will be emphasised in a number of later chapters, NWLC and productivity changes are not likely to be independent since some cost components, particularly within the non-obligatory category, are designed to enhance the productive performance of the workforce. To a limited extent, therefore, real cost increases may be reflected later in productivity increases. This apart, it seems difficult to avoid speculating that international differences in changes of NWLCs per unit of output of these magnitudes cannot auger well for the competitive position of economies like the UK relative to those like the US.

A direct comparison of the type of NWLC ratio shown in Table 3.1

Table 3.3 *Real labour costs and productivity: mineral-oil refining, textiles and total manufacturing industries, FRG, 1972–81*

Year	*Industry*[a]	*Total hourly labour costs*[b] *(1)*	*Total hourly NWLCs*[b] *(2)*	*(2) as % of (1) (3)*	*Productivity*[c] *(4)*	*(1) as % of (4) (5)*	*(2) as % of (4) (6)*
1972	Mineral-oil refining	15.8	4.5	28.3	177.5	8.9	2.5
	Textiles	8.5	2.4	28.6	11.6	73.3	20.7
	All manufacturing	11.1	3.3	29.6	16.5	67.3	20.0
1975	Mineral-oil refining	19.0	7.3	38.3	198.8	9.6	3.7
	Textiles	10.0	3.9	33.9	13.8	72.5	28.3
	All manufacturing	12.7	4.2	32.9	18.6	68.3	22.6
1978	Mineral-oil refining	25.7	9.9	38.4	243.5	10.6	4.1
	Textiles	11.6	3.6	30.7	15.8	73.4	22.8
	All manufacturing	15.2	5.0	32.8	21.7	70.0	23.0
1981	Mineral-oil refining	27.7	10.9	39.5	200.0	13.9	5.5
	Textiles	12.4	4.0	31.7	17.2	72.1	23.3
	All manufacturing	16.6	5.5	33.3	23.7	70.0	23.2

[a] Firms with 10+ employees.
[b] DMs in 1970 prices.
[c] Value of output per person hour in DMs in 1970 prices.

Sources: *Eurostat*: see Table A2.1; Rolf Krengel *et al.*, Produktionsvolumen und -potential, 'Produktionsfaktoren des Bergbaus und der verarbeitenden Gewerbes in der Bundesrepublik Deutschland' (Berlin: Deutsches Institut für Wirtschaftsforschung, 1972, 1975, 1978, 1981).

with NWLCs per unit of output is made in Table 3.3. The ratios are presented for mineral-oil refining, textile and total manufacturing industries in the FRG between 1972 and 1981. Mineral-oil refining is one of the most capital-intensive industries while the textile industry has a relatively high labour intensity. In 1972, both industries had the same proportions of NWLCs to total labour costs (see column 3), lying quite near to the average for all manufacturing industry. After 1972, this proportion rose to well above the average in mineral-oil refining while, in textiles, it remained (apart from in 1975) below the average. This ratio alone, however, gives a somewhat misleading picture of the general 'significance' of the growth of NWLCs in these industries. When (as in column 6) hourly NWLCs are expressed as a ratio of the per-hour value of output, the foregoing impression of the relative cost positions requires modification. Again, in 1972, the textiles' ratio lies quite near the average for total manufacturing whereas the ratio in mineral-oil refining is *one-eighth* of the average. This gap is narrowed somewhat by 1981, at which time the textiles' ratio remains near the manufacturing average while that in mineral-oil refining has increased to between one-quarter and one-fifth of the average.[4] Of course, given the information in column 3, the increase in NWLCs per unit of output in mineral-oil refining is greater than the equivalent increase in terms of total labour costs (see column 5). In summary, for both NWLC ratios (columns 3 and 6), the increases in NWLCs are more apparent in mineral-oil refining. However, in terms of unit output, the costs lie well below the industrial average throughout the period in this industry. It would not be surprising if these sorts of industrial differences in the relative levels and changes of the NWLC ratios were reflected in wide variations in industrial economic responsiveness to changes in the costs. One policy aspect of this possibility is discussed with respect to worksharing in Chapter 9.

For reasons that are discussed in the next chapter and beyond, it would be expected that the proportion of non-obligatory social welfare costs to total labour costs will relate positively to skill level. On the other hand, it may be anticipated, though less strongly, that the relationship between statutory welfare contributions and skill will run in the opposite direction. As explained with reference to Tables 2.6 and 2.7, the vast majority of lower-skilled workers receive earnings below statutory ceiling levels and so the full impact of statutory payments will pertain. These expectations are borne out in Table 3.4, which shows, for the UK and FRG, statutory and non-obligatory contributions by manual and non-manual workers (as a rough skill disaggregation) between 1972/73 and 1981. In both countries, the sizes of the non-obligatory ratios for non-manual workers average about twice those for manual and, although the orders of magnitude are less,

Table 3.4 *Statutory and non-obligatory social welfare contributions as percentage of total labour costs by manual and non-manual workers: UK and FRG manufacturing industries*[a], *1972/3–81*

Year	UK				FRG			
	Statutory		Non-obligatory		Statutory		Non-obligatory	
	Manual	Non-manual	Manual	Non-manual	Manual	Non-manual	Manual	Non-manual
1972/1973	5.9	4.6	2.4	7.1	16.3	11.9	1.2	2.8
1975	7.2	6.1	3.5	7.8	17.0	13.0	1.2	2.4
1978	9.3	7.9	5.0	8.8	17.9	13.6	2.6	5.7
1981	9.7	8.5	5.5	8.8	17.9	13.3	2.7	5.5

[a] Firms with 50+ employess
Source: *Eurostat*: see Table A2.1.

the statutory manual ratios are clearly higher than those of the non-manual. In a much more detailed industrial breakdown of NWLCs for the UK and FRG in 1975 (see Bell *et al.*, 1980), these patterns are shown to hold strongly in almost every industry.

Breaking down the ratios of statutory and non-obligatory social welfare costs to total labour costs by size of firm would be expected to reveal opposing trends. The statutory ratios should be negatively related to firm size. The reason for this is that, since average earnings are positively related to firm size (for UK and FRG evidence, see Bell *et al.*, 1980), then smaller firms will have proportionately more workers below statutory ceiling limits thereby increasing statutory contributions relative to wage costs. There are several reasons, on the other hand, to expect that larger firms will be more inclined to incur relatively higher proportions of non-obligatory expenditures (see below and Chapter 10). At the three levels of size disaggregation per-

Table 3.5 *Japanese social welfare costs as percentage of total labour costs by size of firm: all industries, 1978*

Size of firm (nos of employees)	Social welfare costs: Statutory	Social welfare costs: Non-obligatory	Total
30 – 99	7.3	4.0	11.3
100 – 299	7.1	4.9	12.0
300 – 999	6.8	6.3	13.1
1000 – 4999	6.7	7.5	14.2
5000+	6.6	6.8	13.4

Source: Japanese *Year Book of Labour Statistics*: see Table A2.1.

Table 3.6 *Indirect costs[a] as percentage of total labour costs by size of firm: UK and FRG, 1978*

Size of firm (nos of employees)	*UK*	*FRG*
10 – 49	24.8	35.2
50 – 99	25.3	36.6
100 – 199	26.3	37.7
200 – 499	27.1	38.8
500 – 999	28.1	40.1
1000 +	29.3	43.0

[a] Indirect costs comprise all NWLCs *plus* other bonuses.
Source: *Eurostat*: see Table A2.1.

mitted by the Eurostat statistics (10–49, 50+ and 1000+ employees), Bell *et al.* (1980) show that both the statutory and non-obligatory cost expectations hold for almost every manufacturing industry in the UK and FRG in 1975. By way of confirmation, Table 3.5 reveals the same relationships in the ratios for five size-groups of Japanese industries in 1978. Note that the *total* Japanese social welfare proportions (except for the largest firm size) are positively related to firm size, indicating that the trend in the non-obligatory proportions is stronger than the opposing statutory trend. This would also seem to be the case in the UK and FRG, where the ratio of NWLCs (all categories, including the relatively small item, bonuses) to total labour costs clearly rises with firm size (see Table 3.6).

One major reason for an expected positive relationship between the non-obligatory social welfare ratio and firm size relates to an important component of this NWLC category – that is, deferred fringe

Table 3.7 *Proportions of firms and employees with private old age pensions by size of firm: FRG, 1973 and 1976*

Size of firm (nos of employees)	*Firms* 1973	*Firms* 1976	*Employees* 1973	*Employees* 1976
10 – 49	18.3	26.7	11.3	17.6
50 – 99	45.8	55.1	26.9	31.9
100 – 199	53.7	69.2	36.5	44.1
200 – 499	69.4	83.9	55.8	62.6
500 – 999	80.7	93.1	65.0	77.3
1000 – 4999	} 86.2	98.6	} 86.4	88.9
5000 +		99.3		90.1

Source: Reinhard Clemens and Helmut Wollrab, '*Zur Entwicklung der Personal- und Personalnebenkosten*' (Göttingen: Otto Swartz & Co., 1981).

benefit compensation. There exist scale economies in the company purchase of, for example, insurance and pension cover; larger companies are not only better able to spread the fixed costs of setting up and administering the various funds but they can also obtain, through group discounts, lower per-worker charges for fund management. Supporting evidence is provided in Table 3.7, which shows a steeply rising trend in the proportion of firms and employees covered by private pension schemes by size of firm in the FRG. For *all* firm sizes, a noticeable rise in both types of coverage between 1973 and 1976 is also indicated.

The link between unionism and fringe benefit compensation is dealt with in Chapters 4 and 10. On the average, unionised firms pay a higher proportion of fringe benefits within total compensation than non-unionised firms, and a recent literature has grown that has developed and tested theories to explain this phenomenon. Since the percentage of unionised firms grows with firm size, as clearly illustrated in the cases of the FRG (metal working industry) and Japan in Tables 3.8 and 3.9 respectively, then work in this area may go some way towards accounting for the distribution of non-obligatory social welfare payments by size of firm. As discussed at a later stage, an influential approach towards examining union fringe benefit bargaining is the median voter model. This predicts that unions will tend to represent the interest of members with relatively long job tenure. Such workers are likely to have a preference for fringes, particularly in the form of deferred compensation (Nealey, 1963). Now, it might be expected that the median voter explanation of fringe benefit payments would apply particularly forcibly to workers in larger firms because such workers have longer job tenure due, for example, to greater opportunities for internal mobility.

Table 3.8 *Degree of unionisation by size of firm in the metal working industry: FRG, 1978*

Size of firm (nos of employees)	*Degree of unionisation (%)*	
	Manual	*Non-manual*
1 – 49	51.6	20.4
50 – 99	49.9	20.0
100 – 499	54.3	23.9
500 – 999	60.9	28.4
1000 – 4999	67.0	29.8
5000 +	80.6	39.3

Source: IG Metall, *Results of the Works Council Elections of 1978* (Frankfurt am Main: 1980).

Table 3.9 *Degree of unionisation by size of firm: Japan, 1976*

Size of firm (nos of employees)	*Degree of unionisation (%)*
1 – 29	1
30 – 99	12
100 – 499	40
500 +	71

Source: A. Ernst *et al.*, *Japans unvollkommene Beschäftigung* (Hamburg: Institut für Asienkunde, 1980), p. 31.

NOTES

1 Although activity rates *after* the compulsory age of retirement remain high and are comparable to those in other OECD countries for the population aged 55–65. The seniority-based wage system is effective up to the compulsory retirement age, while wages for workers in the 55 and older age groups fall off quite appreciably compared to the trend in the under-55 groups.

2 Note that the US figures cover only a very limited area (see note (d), Table 3.1) and obviously cannot be compared with the other three countries. Also, the Japanese figures, unlike those for the FRG and UK, include recruitment costs.

3 An even stronger US performance is apparent in the case of *direct* real wage costs per unit of output. This can be inferred from Table 3.1, which reveals that total NWLCs have risen relative to total labour costs in all countries. In fact, over this period, real wage costs in the USA have fallen by roughly 10 per cent, contrasting with rises of roughly 30 and 5 per cent in the UK and FRG, respectively.

4 Although it is not shown here, there is a general tendency (as far as FRG and UK data are concerned) for the proportions of NWLCs to total labour costs to be relatively high in the more capital-intensive industries with, not unexpectedly, the same industries exhibiting low levels of NWLCs relative to net value added.

REFERENCES

Bell, D. N. F., R. A. Hart and F. X. Kirwan (1980), *Non-Wage Labour Costs, their Importance and Effects: A Comparative Study of the United Kingdom, Germany and Italy*, Programme of Research and Actions on the Development of the Labour Market, Brussels: Commission of the European Communities, Study No. 78/14.

Cole, R. E. (1972), 'Permanent employment in Japan: facts and fantasies', *Industrial Relations Review*, 26, 615–630.

Nealey, M (1963), 'Pay and benefit preference', *Industrial Relations*, 3, 17–28.

Patrick, H. and H. Rosovsky (eds) (1976), *Asia's New Giant*, Washington DC: The Brookings Institution.

4 Why Do Firms Incur Such Costs?

The previous two chapters have established the importance of non-wage labour costs within the average firm's total labour cost considerations. With perhaps a somewhat slow adjustment lag, the growth in the postwar significance of these costs has been accompanied by a growth in the economics literature devoted to analysing their role in the functioning of labour markets. Accordingly, the following six chapters attempt to present some of the major developments that have taken place. An essential starting point is to establish the reasons why firms incur NWLCs and it is on this aspect of the subject that most of the present chapter concentrates. The main explanations are ordered under the headings 'human capital', 'collective bargaining' and 'technical' in sections 4.1, 4.2 and 4.3, respectively. However, one category of NWLC, indeed one of the quantitatively most important, is in no sense incurred by the firm but, rather, is imposed on it. This is broadly covered by the 'obligatory social welfare' cost heading in Table 3.1. The study of the growth of legislatively imposed costs on firms constitutes a vast subject in its own right and we shall be content to outline, in section 4.4, some of the more important features and trends. This section is followed by discussion of a highly related topic in section 4.5. This concerns the ability of the firm to pass on obligatory social welfare taxes in the form of compensating wage differentials or price mark-ups. In order to gain a flavour of the subject matter of subsequent chapters, the discussion throughout the chapter is also intended as a vehicle for introducing some of the economic issues that are to be examined in more depth later.

4.1 NON-WAGE LABOUR COSTS AS HUMAN CAPITAL INVESTMENTS

Human capital theory has provided the most influential framework within which to analyse both why firms incur certain non-wage labour costs and the labour market implications of the costs once incurred. The foundations for most subsequent developments in the field were laid in the seminal work of Oi (1962) and Becker (1964).

A firm invests in a worker's human capital in order to achieve a higher expected marginal value product discounted over his/her expected future working lifetime in the firm. Expenditures on training and retraining programmes provide an obvious example of such investment. A relatively high proportion of training would be expected to be firm-specific, since more general training would also enhance a worker's marginal product in other firms. In part, hiring expenditures also enable firms to increase the marginal value product of new hires. Careful search on the labour market combined with well-designed interview/examination techniques and, possibly, probationary trial periods of employment help to reduce the proportion of workers unsuited to the firm's organisational and technological make-up. Careful selection involves an element of specific human capital creation as the firm will attempt to match candidates to its own particular idiosyncrasies. Almost certainly, however, hiring costs involve major general investments since there are likely to be significant overlaps among firms in their views concerning the qualities of potential recruits that are deemed to be most desirable. Other aspects of hiring involve no direct investment in human capital. Personnel departments are involved in the general administration of the legislative and internal details associated with hiring, and firing, that occur irrespective of the mode of selection in operation.

Introducing training and hiring costs into the traditional economic treatment of the optimising firm's behaviour has immediate fundamental implications. Classical economic theory treats labour input as a variable factor of production, and equilibrium for a profit-maximising firm operating in competitive product and factor markets is given by:

$$v_{\mathrm{mp}} = p.mp_{\mathrm{L}} = w \tag{4.1}$$

where v_{mp} is the value of the marginal product of labour, p is product price, mp_{L} is the marginal physical product of labour and w is the wage rate. An unanticipated fall in product demand, for example, reduces product price and equilibrium is maintained by a labour force reduction, assuming diminishing marginal productivity.

In the classical, short-run model, on the other hand, capital is usually differentiated from labour by treating it as a fixed factor input with zero adjustment potential. However, the inclusion of hiring and training expenditures introduces an element of capital into labour input and this consideration led Oi and Becker to treat labour as a 'quasi-fixed' factor of production. To simplify matters, assume that the firm incurs hiring and training costs, represented by k, only in the initial period. The new profit-maximising condition, with respect to hiring an additional worker, can be written in terms of the firm equating total costs and total revenues, that is:

$$k = \sum_{t=0}^{T-1} (p_t mp_t - w_t)(1 + r_t)^{-t} \tag{4.2}$$

where, ignoring rehiring possibilities, T is the worker's expected period of employment in the firm and, for the t'th period, mp_t is marginal product and r_t is the discount rate. In equilibrium, the firm equates the present value of its fixed labour costs with the discounted present value of the net (of wages) marginal value product. In order to satisfy (4.2), the firm must pay a wage, in one or more periods, that is *less* than the value of the marginal product. If, for example, the firm was to follow the classical equilibrium condition in (4.1) for each t'th period, it would not maximise profits since, for some of the workforce, the returns from fixed labour investments would be insufficient to amortise the initial investment expenditures.

For simplicity, assume that the firm forms single-valued expectations of the future quantities in (4.2); that is:

$$\mathrm{E}(p_t) = p^*,\ \mathrm{E}(mp_t) = mp^*,\ \mathrm{E}(w_t) = w^* \text{ for } t = 0, \ldots, T. \tag{4.3}$$

Incorporating these expectations in (4.2) gives:

$$v_{\mathrm{mp}^*} = p^* mp^* = w^* + R \tag{4.4}$$

where

$$R = \frac{k}{\sum_{t=0}^{T-1} (1 + r)^{-t}}. \tag{4.5}$$

R is the quasi-periodic rent or 'the surplus which must be earned by each worker in order to amortize the initial fixed employment costs' (Oi, 1962, p. 541).

The main difference between (4.4) and (4.1) is that, on the average, the firm sets the employment level so that marginal product is higher than the wage rate by an amount equivalent to the periodic rent, R. The inclusion of R in (4.4) serves to modify the employment predictions of the classical model following demand changes. Suppose there is an unanticipated *permanent* product demand fall. Hiring and training costs become sunk costs and exert no influence on short-run decisions. Given an assumption that wage rates remain unchanged, two possibilities can occur. First, the lower expected value of the marginal product may be such that $v_{mp^*} < w^*$ in (4.4). In this event, employment would fall in the short run by an amount sufficient to equate v_{mp^*} and w^*. At the margin, some workers would be retained by the firm despite the fact that their marginal value product is not sufficient to cover the periodic rent. Employment will fall further in the longer term since the firm will not replace employment losses through natural wastage until the equilibrium condition in (4.4) is restored. Secondly, the lower expected value of the marginal product may be such that $w^* \leq v_{mp^*} \leq w^* + R$. Here, there will be no short-run employment fall since the receipt of part of the return to sunk investments is better than none at all, which would be the case if workers are (permanently) laid off. If, on the other hand, the product demand fall is expected to be only *temporary* then the firm may be willing to retain certain types of worker despite a fall in marginal product below the wage. The firm will weigh the expected cost of this action against the loss of human capital investment in the event of a laid-off worker finding a new employer and thus being unavailable for re-hire when demand picks up once again. In general, the expected cost of layoff will be higher, and thus the probability of retention higher, the greater is the job specificity of the worker concerned. We shall see shortly, however, that this statement is tempered to the degree that the worker shares the return to the specific investment.

An immediate implication of this analysis is that labour factors with relatively high degrees of fixity, as determined by the size of the ratio $R/(R + w^*)$, would be expected to exhibit relatively low employment fluctuations resulting from given unanticipated product demand changes. As will be discussed later, especially in Chapters 6 and 7, this has important implications for the cyclical analysis of labour markets.

In assessing the value of the expected wage, one of the firm's prime considerations will be the amount of specific investment endowed in a given labour unit. The firm will not pay for completely general training since a resulting increment to marginal product is also a potential increment to other firms if the worker quits. The net value of general training is zero, since the worker could effectively raise the wage rate by selling, or threatening to sell, the training elsewhere. Indeed, assuming no other mobility costs, purely generally trained workers would be paid a wage relative to their opportunity wage or the wage they could obtain elsewhere. As trainees, such workers would be prepared to pay for their own general training since, as it enhances their future marginal product in many firms, they will perceive it as an investment in the growth of their future wage stream. During the training period, therefore, they would be willing to accept a wage equivalent to their opportunity wage minus the total cost of the training. Of somewhat more interest is the expected wage of workers with significant specific human capital investments. Such workers would be very reluctant to pay all their own training costs. If they did so then, during a demand downturn, they would be more readily laid off by the firm since they would be regarded in effect as a variable input factor. Further, they would face a wage reduction given that their opportunity marginal product would be less than their marginal product with the firm. This is an unlikely outcome, however, for there is a great incentive for the firm to share the return to specific investment with the worker in the form of a wage premium. If the firm pays a premium, its expected wage would increase but so would the expected tenure of the worker, thereby reducing the periodic rent. The firm will equate the marginal increase in the expected wage with the expected marginal reduction in the periodic rent. It follows that the level of wage premium for any given worker would be expected to be positively related to both his/her degree of specificity and perceived propensity to quit.

Another aspect of the firm's possible wage strategy in the face of fixed hiring and training expenditures is provided by the implicit wage contract literature (see Okun, 1981). It may be in the firm's and the worker's mutual interest to share the quasi-rent in the form of a seniority-based payments structure. For example, as discussed later in section 6.4, both sides may enter into a long-term implicit contract under a dual wage structure. In their initial employment period, new recruits accept a lower wage that reflects their agreement to pay part of specific fixed labour investments. Established workers are paid a wage premium that represents their share of the quasi-rent accruing to the investments. This latter wage would lie between the marginal value product of established workers and the wage they would earn if they were new recruits elsewhere.Under this type of implicit agreement, workers signal their long-term intentions to remain with the firm by accepting the lower starting wage. Firms for their part reveal their intentions of a long-term employment relationship by their commitment to pay a part of the fixed investments.

The likelihood of the firm and the worker sharing the quasi-rent has a significant implication for the choice of adjustment mode to a fall in product demand. Oi and Becker concentrate on quantity adjustment, whereas, as pointed out by Hashimoto (1975), the position may arise whereby both parties would jointly optimise their returns by agreeing to a price-adjustment formulation. As discussed in Chapter 7, it is possible that a wage-reduction response to an unanticipated product demand fall may serve to avoid a non-optimum separation.

While the concept of the periodic rent has proved to be analytically important, there remain formidable problems, often unrecognised in the literature, over precisely how the firm estimates the returns to specific investments. At a point in time, the returns to a given specific investment may be represented by a density function. Higher standard errors around the expected value would reflect greater uncertainty over changes in product demand, process and product innovation, work organisation, technological endowment, etc., affecting the firm and other firms. In Chapter 7, an attempt in the literature to integrate this type of uncertainty over the size of the quasi-rent into the analysis of wage flexibility is examined.

The high, and probably asymmetrical, information costs to the firm and its workforce involved in estimating returns to specific investment may induce each side to signal its intentions of a long-term commitment by entering into a special type of implicit or explicit contractual agreement. Perhaps the obvious type is one where compensation is deferred, rising progressively with the length of job tenure. Specific models of deferred compensation are discussed in Chapters 6 and 10. The main point of interest here is that one means of achieving such a payment system is for the firm to pay fringe benefits, which comprise a combination of fixed and variable NWLCs, in the form of deferred entitlement. An obvious example is that of a private firm pension plan that is designed to penalise employees who quit during some pre-specified period. Deferred fringes may not only reduce labour turnover, with its associated dismissal and rehiring costs, but also, as part of a general seniority-based deferred compensation system, encourage greater productive effort among younger workers (see Lazear, 1981). The firm may also unilaterally invest in a wide range of social and recreational facilities, all closely linked to the firm, which are designed to imbue an identity, even loyalty, of the worker to the firm. Again, those fringes that are intended to improve the general working environment – such as recreation, canteen and social facilities, or the special design and layout of workplaces – are likely to provide the firm with two types of return. Labour turnover will be reduced through fewer quits and the improved psychic return to workers may well be reflected in greater work application and effort.

In all, the firm undertakes three broad types of human capital investment, which we may label *selection, improvement* and *protection* investments. Selection investment covers expenditure on search and screening techniques designed to increase the marginal value product of new hires. Worker dismissal costs would also enter under this heading to the extent that the firm may voluntarily commit itself to redundancy payments in order to allow greater flexibility over the choice and timing of its firing strategy. Improvement investment involves specific training programmes designed to increase labour's value product over and above its pre-entry endowment. Protection investment covers a wide spectrum of payments designed to safeguard the previous two types of investment by increasing the expected working lifetime in the firm of those labour units endowed with relatively high specific human capital. In so far as these latter investments improve the 'quality' of working life, they are also likely to improve labour's marginal product; work application and effort are not likely to be independent of psychic returns.

As we have already mentioned in relation to hiring costs, the firm would probably regard a proportion of its per-period outlay of expenditure on such investments as being exogenously determined, at least in the short run. For example, the current given level of technology employed by the firm will help to determine certain minimum requirements over the type of new hires and/or the degree to which they should be trained. Yet there is likely to be a significant choice or endogenous element in such expenditures. Beyond the minimum investments determined by the firm's given technical and organisational characteristics, the firm has discretion to vary the investments to levels consistent with perceived inter-temporal optimisation of returns. The ability of the firm to affect labour productivity by varying the level of these investments has implications for production and factor demand models that incorporate quasi-fixed labour costs. We shall return to this topic in several places throughout the text.

Allowing for a price as well as a quantity adjustment response to unforeseen product demand changes helps to enrich the Becker/Oi framework. It also broadens its usefulness as a means of understanding aspects of labour market behaviour, especially in the area of cyclical wage responsiveness (see section 7.2). However, the explicit recognition that there exist different modes of quantity adjustment itself has even more far-reaching consequences. The firm has the possibility of changing both the stock *and utilisation* of the labour input to demand and factor price changes. Given increases in hiring and training costs, *ceteris paribus,* then the possibility of substituting more average hours per worker for fewer workers may be particularly appealing to the firm since the former are independent of such NWLCs (although this is not true of other types of fixed cost, as discussed in section 4.3 and Chapter 5). Important papers by Rosen (1968) and Nadiri and Rosen (1969) demonstrate the theoretical and empirical necessity, given labour's quasi-fixity, of modifying the work of Oi and Becker to accommodate the labour utilisation dimension. This aspect of the subject has provided not only important developments in labour demand and production theory but also in a fairly wide range of related applications. These are discussed in the chapters that follow.

4.2 NON-WAGE LABOUR COSTS AND COLLECTIVE BARGAINING

Circumstantial evidence is presented in Chapter 3 to suggest that there is a positive relationship between the proportion of non-wage labour costs to total labour costs and the degree of unionisation. The desire by firms to incur human capital investments may be mutually consistent with a preference by workers to receive part of their compensation package in the form of non-wage payments and, moreover, such a preference may be better expressed through union representation. Of the NWLCs itemised in Table 2.1, non-obligatory costs would obviously be deemed to be the area in which both sides would have the greatest common interest. Here, we would clearly include such items as private insurance and pension schemes.

In the case of the US economy, more concrete evidence supports a positive association between the proportion of fringe payments within total compensation and the degree of unionisation. Using data from a detailed Bureau of Labor Statistics survey undertaken in 1974, Mitchell (1980) estimates that the union wage for non-office workers in all non-farm industries exceeds the non-union wage by 52 per cent. However, this premium is increased to 67 per cent when total compensations, including all fringe benefits, are compared. This difference persists when manufacturing and non-manufacturing sectors are separated. In both sectors, the union establishments receive over three times the level of private fringe benefits paid to the non-union establishments. While such information is merely suggestive of a direct union influence, Freeman (1981) provides econometric support for the hypothesis that unions raise the proportion of fringes within total compensation. In particular, he finds that unionism is especially associated with the importance of deferred fringe payments that favour senior workers, such as pensions, insurance cover and vacation pay.

A desired increase by an employee in the proportion of fringes within a time unit of total compensation is discussed by Freeman in terms of the wage that would be forgone in exchange. This is referred to as the supply price of fringes. The higher the firm perceives the supply price to be, then the greater the incentive to increase the share of fringes within total compensation. How might the collective action of unions raise the supply price above that of individual, non-union members? Freeman's central explanation lays great stress on the trade union in its role as a political institution. A prime objective is the desire to win the support of the majority of its members. Since 'voting' or paying union dues is a recurrent activity, the union is likely to link its political objectives to the aspirations of those workers with the longest expected lengths of stay within the firm, or firms, in which it has an influence. On the average, such workers will be older workers since they have the longest expected rates of job tenure (see Hall, 1982). Not only do older workers exhibit a greater preference for fringes anyway (Nealey, 1963), they also stand to gain relatively if their propensity to remain in their job is rewarded by fringes with embedded deferred increments.

For individual workers who are interested in receiving fringes, there may appear to be a marked advantage in negotiating a package of benefits through union collective bargaining. The information costs to the individual involved in estimating the expected future yields of pension plans, health schemes and so on in order to assemble an optimum package may be prohibitively high. Combining collectively, through a union, to buy the information is a far more feasible proposition. For the individual firm that, for reasons mentioned above, shows a propensity to pay deferred compensation, the role of unions may well be considered to be a positive one. By enforcing seniority rights, unions *enable* the firm to defer more compensation without increasing the risk to workers.

These and other arguments (see Freeman, 1981; Mabry, 1973) underpin Mitchell's observation of an increase in the union/non-union pay ratios when fringes are added to wages. Thus, especially in the relatively skilled union sectors, examples exist of firms and workers finding it in their common interest to increase the proportion of non-wages, in the form of fringe benefits, within total compensation. In these cases, estimating the potential level of fringes involves the construction of a bargaining model in which both demand and supply variables play an interactive role. Indeed, unravelling demand and supply influences involves solving an inherent simultaneity problem, which has been largely ignored in the literature. To what extent is long job tenure due to high fringes paid by firms as protection investments and to what extent are high fringes due to unions bargaining on behalf of members with long tenure? This, however, is not particularly important for our present purposes. It is sufficient to note that, especially in the categories 'payments for days not worked' and 'customary (etc.) costs' (see Table 2.1), it is likely that a proportion of many firms' contributions is determined by the bargaining behaviour of unions. We return to this topic in Chapter 10.

Apart from fringe benefits, an important element of NWLCs falls largely within the domain of collective bargaining decisions. This concerns another type of payment for time not worked and involves, in particular, agreed stoppages *during* the working day. The most common example is time allocated for rest periods and/or tea-breaks. Other, more specific, examples include paid time-periods allocated to workers' journey to the workplace, cleaning and changing, attending union/works council meetings and stoppages due to adverse weather conditions. As we shall see later (Chapter 6), such costs have been specifically linked to arguments concerning the returns to labour services in production function estimation.

4.3 CAPITAL AND ORGANISATIONAL CONSTRAINTS

As previously mentioned, hiring and training costs are likely to be determined in part by the firm's existing capital endowment expressed in terms of both the capital/labour ratio and the vintage of capital. The necessity to employ minimum skill levels of labour ensures that an unavoidable level of these costs is incurred. Comparable constraints may well be imposed by the firm's organisational structure. Similarly, production set-up costs, a part of fixed NWLCs, are likely to be determined partly by capital and organisational constraints.[1] However, the economic interest in this aspect of NWLCs is perhaps reduced by the fact that, in any case, labour costs in highly capitalised industries are low relative to net value added (for example, see Table 3.3). Costs associated with capital and organisational constraints become more interesting when judged in terms of worker-adjustment costs given, for example, unanticipated changes in product demand. Such adjustment costs are discussed in some detail by Soligo (1966).

An example of adjustment costs occurs when there is some degree of fixed proportionality between labour and capital, combined with capital indivisibility, and the firm faces an unexpected demand change. Short-run costs arise because the achievement of optimum or desired levels of labour input is constrained to await such times as a change in the stock of capital can be effected. Another example, which is somewhat analogous, involves attempts to change the organisational structure of the workforce given either the introduction of a new product/production process or the attempt to realise economies. Overcoming the old order and establishing the new may well involve costs associated with retraining, firing and hiring and general labour force inertia. Soligo emphasises that these and other costs are likely to be higher for non-production as opposed to production workers. The skills, organisation and knowhow associated with non-production workers often take longer to develop and so it is more costly to bring about changes in their work practices. Also, in general, non-production activities contain fewer labour divisibilities than production work.

These and similar types of adjustment cost constitute a fixed production input in much the same way as the stock of capital. As pointed out by Okun (1981, p. 17), however, in many instances the labour overheads do not arise from sunk costs 'but rather from a production function in which capital and labour are complementary (and not substitutive) in the short run'.

Quasi-fixed NWLCs are expressed only in terms of *per-worker* costs. As suggested by Hart and Robb (1983),equivalent hourly operating costs do exist that vary only with average hours worked per worker and that arise, principally, for exogenous technical-scale reasons. Thus, for example, if the firm wishes to extend the work week, then it must incur the extra cost of maintaining an adequate working environment. Obvious cost items here include heating and lighting, but a whole range of other activities such as security services and canteen facilities might also be included. Some attention is given to hourly operating costs in the following chapter.

4.4 DIRECT AND INDIRECT LEGISLATIVE INFLUENCES

As is clear from Table 3.1, statutory social welfare provision constitutes the major, or joint-major, non-wage labour cost to the firm. Moreover, the general growth of NWLCs owes much to this item. The reasons for the growth embrace an enormous subject area, intimately tied up with the analysis of the development of the welfare state in general, which is well beyond the scope of this book. It will suffice here to mention four of the more important features.

(i) Antecedents and Long-term Trend

Since the 1940s there has been a substantial growth both in the number of countries providing each main type of social welfare provision (see, for example, US Department of Health and Human Resources, 1979) and in the real worth of individual benefit. The growth in average individual benefit is reflected not only in improving benefit replacement ratios, such as for the retired and the unemployed, but also in increases in benefit eligibility.

Apart from exceptional cases, such as the UK, the main structural foundations of Western countries' programmes were laid down during the Great Depression. Feldstein (1977) highlights two broad design features of current programmes that were specifically drawn up as a reaction to the experiences of that time and, moreover, that reflected contemporaneous changes in economic orthodoxy. First, the schemes were designed to provide a substitute for private saving, given that the depression severely reduced the lifetime savings of many families. The risks of this happening in the future were to be reduced in the sense that important elements in the motives behind private individual saving, such as against the risk of long illness, industrial injury or unemployment as well as to provide income for retirement, would be effectively removed. Second, within a climate of both high and long-term unemployment, benefits to the retired and the unemployed would have the beneficial results of replacing lost savings and stimulating consumption, which, through well-known Keynesian channels, would eventually filter through into new job creation.[2]

Until relatively recent times, both governments and individuals have appeared to find it in their mutual interest to expand considerably beyond the degree and breadth of coverage in the depression years. Feldstein goes on to enumerate a number of apparent advantages in extending the programmes both to the individual and to the government. For example, many individuals may find it difficult to purchase annuities on the private market equivalent to certain social welfare provisions provided by the state. Also, statutory state schemes help to circumvent the high information costs to the individual of choosing equivalent private insurance cover in complex markets. In that individuals, collectively, may choose a range of cover that is similar to the social welfare programme anyway, then the economy may realise a net efficiency gain. Another popular rationale for the growth of these schemes (see, for example, Pechman, 1977) runs as follows. Whatever the initial motivation, social welfare programmes have developed away from the simple insurance principle. Beneficiaries have tended to receive significantly higher benefits than their tax payments, allowing for a reasonable rate of return. One major reason for this is that governments have tried to maintain the real worth of benefits, even in times of very high inflation. The high demands on the schemes have usually meant that firms' and workers' contributions are not accumulated and invested in order to be paid as future benefits but merely used as payment for current benefit. Thus, it is argued, social welfare programmes have provided a simple taxation device to finance government social programmes.

(ii) Demographic Influences

Given the social security structures that have evolved, one relatively recent development, which has occurred throughout most OECD countries, has tended to increase the real trend of firm/worker contributions and will almost certainly exert a long-term future influence. This concerns demographic changes and their effects on pension contributions. The issue of most concern is a reduction in the ratio of active to inactive population, primarily due to an increase in the proportion of the total population above the age of retirement. Table 4.1 illustrates the changes in this proportion for our four countries. With

Table 4.1 *Population aged 65 years and over as a percentage of the total labour force, 1965 – 79*

Country	*1965*	*1970*	*1975*	*1979*
FRG	26.0	29.8	33.9	35.9
Japan	12.9	14.2	16.5	18.3
UK	25.8	28.5	30.3	31.2
USA	23.9	23.4	23.7	23.5

Source: OECD, *Labour Force Statistics* (Paris: various volumes).

the exception of the USA,[3] there was a significant increase between 1965 and 1979. Moreover, in most countries this proportion is expected to grow considerably.

The problem is well illustrated by Japan, which, although at the high end of the spectrum, provides a generally representative example of a common trend. Beyond the picture presented in Table 4.1, there are substantial forecasted growth rates of the numbers in the Japanese age cohorts beyond the official age of retirement (55–60, although activity rates remain high up to 65) for the period 1980 – 95 (see Shimada, 1980). On the other hand, much lower growth rates, some of which are negative, are forecast for the cohorts between 15 and 40 years of age. The pension insurance system in Japan is somewhat complicated, embracing eight different schemes (see Hiraishi, 1980, for details). However, there are two dominant schemes that cover about 90 per cent of the total insured population and one of these, the Employees' Pension Insurance Scheme, will suffice to represent the general problem of the growing financial burden of retirement. This scheme is financed principally through contributions by employees and employers on a 50 – 50 basis. In 1979, contribution rates were 9.1 per cent of wages for insured male workers. In 1977, the number of recipients of old age pension under the scheme reached 1.4 million, which represented roughly seven times the number of recipients of corresponding pensions in 1965. Moreover, it is estimated that, by the year 2010, the proportion of beneficiaries to the number of insured will rise almost five-fold from 1980 and nearly 100-fold from 1960. It is also further estimated that the cost of pensions will rise about 120 – 140-fold between the years 1980 and 2025. Given these estimates, by the twenty-first century the present contribution rate of around 9 per cent of wages will need to rise in excess of 18 per cent in order to cover the cost of the fund. On top of these financial burdens, there also exist *company-specific* retirement allowances, which are large lump-sum payments varying with length of service, type of occupation, education, size of firm and so on. For large firms, such allowances are approximately equivalent to forty regular monthly payments. Perhaps not surprisingly, there is currently a significant move by firms in Japan to increase the compulsory age of retirement.

(iii) Cyclical Features

Of the three important items of social welfare expenditure (i.e. pensions, sickness and unemployment), unemployment insurance financing and, in the case of the FRG, short-time working subsidies (financed from the unemployment insurance fund) are obviously the most cyclically prone to change. In an era of high unemployment in OECD countries and economic forecasts that indicate little medium-term change, pressures for increase in firms' and workers' contributions may be expected to continue. An emphasis on firms' contributions to unemployment insurance funding and its relationship to the existing supply-side orientated literature is the subject of Chapter 8. One way of attempting to mitigate high rates of unemployment is to encourage existing workers to work fewer hours in order to create more jobs. One of the most important recent examples of such an initiative has been the French government's subsidy to obligatory social welfare contributions given to those firms that reduce average hours per worker below the standard work week. In Chapter 9, this type of NWLC subsidy is examined as well as other possibilities of inducing worksharing by government intervention designed to alter the firm's NWLC structure.

(iv) Indirect Legislative Influences

Other areas of government legislation may not be directly intended to change the level of the firm's non-wage labour costs but may, indirectly, achieve this result. Three major examples all relate to the issue of fringe benefits and collective bargaining, discussed in section 4.2 and returned to in Chapter 10. Often fringes are taxed at relatively low marginal rates, if at all. As a result, increases in the marginal rates of income taxes may have the effect, especially in unionised firms, of creating pressure on the firm to switch to a higher proportion of fringes within its total labour cost portfolio. Similar pressure may arise if the government introduces an incomes policy that is less than comprehensive in its attempt to limit the growth of fringe payments. Minimum wage legislation, on the other hand, may have the opposite effect on fringe payments. In order to counter increases in labour costs brought about by the introduction of minimum wages, firms may attempt to reduce fringe payments (see Wessels, 1980).

4.5 BACKWARD AND FORWARD TAX SHIFTING

The example at the end of the last section relates to a much wider issue concerning the impact of obligatory social welfare contributions on the firm's economic activity. Thus, to what extent can the firm pass on the social welfare taxes to its employees through backward and forward shifting? Backward shifting involves restraining wage growth in order to offset tax increases, while forward shifting involves passing on the tax increases in the form of price mark-ups. Brittain (1972) provides the most comprehensive economic analysis of social welfare tax shifting.

The issue of most concern to this text, especially to the developments in Chapters 8 and 9, is the incidence of backward shifting, and the discussion proceeds as if firms do *not* shift the whole burden. Such an assumption is strongly supported by recent econometric evidence. For example, Beach and Balfour (1983) estimate that 45 – 60 per cent of UK firms' share of obligatory welfare taxes is shifted back on to prime-aged male labour and only 14 – 19 per cent on to married women. Hamermesh (1979) estimates that 36 per cent of taxes is shifted back on to adult males in the USA.

Apart from this sort of empirical evidence, two points of emphasis within the structure of the text further limit the importance of this topic. First, much of the analysis here is concerned with factor substitution given relative factor price changes, and tax shifting is not likely to affect substantively the main outcomes. For example, the inducement to the firm to increase labour and/or capital utilisation and reduce the size of its workforce in order to offset increases in social welfare costs that contain high per-worker elements may be expected to occur *despite* tax-shifting possibilities. Such substitution may itself be regarded as a form of shifting the tax to workers in the form of fewer jobs. Indeed, as Beach and Balfour acknowledge in respect of their own study, the general failure by analysts in this area of research to distinguish between workers and hours per worker in labour demand functions may well have produced misleading estimates of demand responses to payroll tax increases. Secondly, although fairly frequent reference is made to longer-term scale effects, the emphasis here on short-run factor substitution limits the impact of tax shifting. In a dynamic analysis of payroll tax incidence, which considers labour demand, labour supply and wage-adjustment responses, Hamermesh (1980) concludes that 'regardless of whether labour bears most of the [payroll] tax increase in the long run, there is a period of at least several years during which labour escapes part of the eventual tax burden and wages fall only part of the way toward their final equilibrium' (p. 763).

NOTES

1 Within a given firm, we might expect a negative correlation between hiring and training investments and set-up costs. For example, greater ability and dexterity in machine use may well reduce work stoppages due to breakdowns as well as the degree of set-up required.
2 That the increasing benefit replacement ratios for the unemployed might have actually succeeded in increasing unemployment rates was a story that did not gain wide popularity until a generation later. We shall touch on this topic in Chapter 8.
3 Indeed, the USA and Canada appear to provide the only instances of OECD countries where the proportion of people over 65 years of age has remained relatively stable over this time-period.

REFERENCES

Beach, C. M. and F. S. Balfour (1983), 'Estimated payroll tax incidence and aggregate demand for labour in the United Kingdom', *Economica,* 50, 35 – 48.

Becker, G. S. (1964), *Human Capital: A Theoretical and Empirical Analysis, with Special Reference to Education,* New York, NY: National Bureau of Economic Research.

Brittain, J. A. (1972), *The Payroll Tax for Social Security,* Washington, DC: The Brookings Institution.

Feldstein, M. (1977), 'Social security' in M.J. Boskin (ed.), *The Crisis on Social Security,* San Francisco, Calif.: Institute for Contemporary Studies.

Freeman, R. B. (1981), 'The effect of unionism on fringe benefits', *Industrial and Labor Relations Review,* 34, 489 – 509.

Hall, R. E. (1982), 'The importance of lifetime jobs in the US economy', *American Economic Review,* 72, 716 – 724.

Hamermesh, D. S. (1979), 'New estimates of the incidence of the payroll tax', *Southern Economic Journal,* 45, 1208 – 1219.

Hamermesh, D. S. (1980), 'Factor market dynamics and the incidence of taxes and subsidies', *Quarterly Journal of Economics,* 95, 751 – 764.

Hart, R. A. and A. L. Robb (1983), 'Production and labour demand functions with endogenous fixed worker costs', Berlin: International Institute of Management, mimeo.

Hashimoto, M. (1975), 'Wage reduction, unemployment and specific human capital', *Economic Inquiry,* 13, 485 – 504.

Hiraishi, N. (1980), *Social Security,* Japanese Industrial Relations Series, Tokyo: The Japanese Institute of Labour.

Lazear, E. P. (1981), 'Agency, earnings profiles, productivity, and hours restrictions', *American Economic Review,* 71, 606 – 620.

Mabry, B. (1973), 'The economics of fringe benefits', *Industrial Relations,* 12, 95 – 106.

Mitchell, D. J. B. (1980), *Wages, Unions and Inflation,* Washington, DC: The Brookings Institution.

Nadiri, M. I. and S. Rosen (1969), 'Interrelated factor demand functions', *American Economic Review,* 59, 457 – 471.

Nealey, S. M. (1963), 'Pay and benefit preference', *Industrial Relations,* 3, 17 – 28.

Oi, W. (1962), 'Labor as a quasi-fixed factor', *Journal of Political Economy,* 70, 538 – 555.

Okun, A. M. (1981), *Prices and Quantities,* Oxford: Basil Blackwell.

Pechman, J. A. (1977), 'The social security system; an overview', in M.J. Boskin (ed.) *The Crisis on Social Security,* San Francisco, Calif.: Institute for Contemporary Studies.

Rosen, S. (1968), 'Short-run employment variation on class-I railroads in the US, 1947 – 1963', *Econometrica,* 36, 511 – 529.

Shimada, H. (1980), *The Japanese Employment System,* Japanese Industrial Relations Series, Tokyo: The Japanese Institute of Labour.

Soligo, R. (1966), 'The short-run relationship between employment and output', *Yale Economic Essays,* 6, 161 – 215.

US Department of Health and Human Resources (1979), *Social Security Programs throughout the World,* Research Report No. 54, Washington, DC: US Government Printing Office.

Wessels, W. J. (1980), 'The effect of minimum wages in the presence of fringe benefits: an expanded model', *Economic Inquiry,* 18, 293 – 313.

5 Factor Substitution and Non-Wage Labour Costs

This chapter investigates the main comparative static theory concerned with the effects of changes in non-wage labour costs and other factor prices on the distribution of workers, hours per worker and the capital stock. It is intended to fulfil two important requirements in the development of the whole text. First, this chapter attempts to underline in a more formal manner why it has been important to distinguish among the various categories of non-wage labour cost in Chapters 2 and 3. Second, it is aimed at providing some useful underpinning of certain theoretical, empirical and policy issues of later chapters.

After setting out the general analytical framework in section 5.1, the chapter develops in the form of variations on a central model theme. In particular, insights will be drawn from simplified sub-models that represent restrictions on the general model construct. A number of these examples relate closely to the existing literature and they will prove to be a helpful basis on which to develop later topics. Section 5.2 presents the five sub-model variations. The first three allow only the labour factor input to vary. The fourth and fifth then investigate, respectively, the consequences of introducing a variable capital stock and changes in worker productivity. The effects on two of the sub-models of allowing for skill differences in the labour input are dealt with in section 5.3. After discussing some consequences of skill disaggregation in the first, and simplest, sub-model, a specific example is then presented for the fourth sub-model, which allows both the labour and capital inputs to vary. A brief section 5.4 concludes the chapter with a discussion of the full general model solution as well as an overview of the sensitivity of the most important results to the imposed restrictions. So as not to clutter the text with unnecessary detail, most technical matters appear in the Appendix to this chapter.

5.1 GENERAL FRAMEWORK

We adopt the dominant micro structure in the literature, which, in this labour demand context, is first formally introduced in Rosen's (1968) paper. Thus, the case is taken of a representative firm that minimises costs subject to a production constraint. For simplicity, the firm is assumed to face a given level of technology and zero variation in stock levels.

Output, Q, is produced according to an instantaneous production function:

$$Q = F(N, h, K, I) \tag{5.1}$$

$$F_i > 0, F_{ii} < 0, F_{ij} > 0 \, (i \neq j), (i, j = 1, \ldots, 4)$$

where N is the number of workers, h is the average hours worked per worker, K is the capital stock and I is an index of productivity per person employed. The restrictions imply positive though diminishing marginal products of factor inputs with positive dependence in cross-marginal products.

Following the sort of argument presented by Feldstein (1967), we allow for the fact that the marginal contribution to labour services of an additional hour differs as between the employment of a new worker or extending the average worktime of an existing worker. Also it is assumed that an increase in labour productivity applies to all manhours of labour. Thus, the labour services function, L, takes the form:

$$L = IG(N, h) \qquad G_N, G_h > 0, \qquad G_{NN}, G_{hh} < 0. \tag{5.2}$$

Average hours are composed of two parts:

$$h = h_s + (h - h_s) \tag{5.3}$$

where h_s is average standard hours, treated as exogenous by the firm, and $(h - h_s)$ is average overtime hours. Several papers (e.g. Brechling, 1965; Rosen, 1968) distinguish among hours that are below, equal to or above h_s. Here, we simplify by assuming that, over the relevant range, the firm's equilibrium level of hours is in the overtime region; thus, in (5.3) $h - h_s > 0$. As discussed by Ehrenberg (1971), this assumption is not very restrictive. There is detailed evidence from micro survey data (see, for example, National Board for Prices and Incomes, 1970; University College, Galway, 1980) that suggests that, in many firms, an important part of overtime work is regularly scheduled. One reason for this concerns fixed NWLCs. These represent, effectively, the 'premium' for employing a new worker in much the same way as overtime premiums represent the costs of extending working hours beyond h_s. Evidence is reported in Chapter 9 that shows that the higher the per capita fixed NWLCs relative to the overtime premium then the greater is the incentive to substitute overtime hours for additional employment.

The firm faces fixed labour costs, z, which vary only with the number of workers. Following Hart and Robb (1983), and related to the discussion in earlier chapters, it is recognised that such costs should be divided into endogenous (z_e) and exogenous (z_x) elements, that is:

$$z = z_e + z_x. \tag{5.4}$$

Following Nadiri and Rosen (1969), a further subdivision of fixed worker costs in (5.4) is warranted, thus:

$$z = \tilde{z} + (q + r)\bar{z} = \tilde{z}_e + \tilde{z}_x + (q + r)(\bar{z}_e + \bar{z}_x) \tag{5.5}$$

where $\tilde{z}$ is the recurring component (e.g. recreation facilities, social welfare payments, holidays) and $\bar{z}$ is the 'once-over' component (e.g. hiring, training and redundancy costs). These latter 'user costs' are adjusted by the quit rate, q, and discounted at a suitable rate of interest, r, to reflect the opportunity cost of capital. Both endogenous and exogenous fixed costs have recurring and 'once-over' elements.

Variable costs, v, are comprised of three parts:

$$v = w_s + w_p + w_n \tag{5.6}$$

where w_s is the standard wage rate, w_p is the premium, or overtime wage rate, and w_n is the variable non-wage cost.

The rates, w_s and w_p are related through the overtime premium, α; that is:

$$w_p = \alpha w_s \quad \alpha > 1. \tag{5.7}$$

As we have seen in Chapters 2 and 3, w_n consists primarily of social welfare contributions that are paid with respect to workers whose wages are below contribution wage ceilings. If ceilings are not crossed, an increased wage automatically ensures an increased contribution. It is assumed here that ceilings exceed w_s and that wages ($w_s + w_p$) of *all* workers in the firm are either above or below each ceiling laid down for each type of social welfare payment. This simplifies matters by ensuring that each type of contribution is assigned totally either to $\tilde{z}_x$ or to w_n. For wages *above* a given ceiling, the contributions constitute a recurring fixed labour cost equal to the wage ceiling multiplied by the contribution rate and, therefore, they are allocated to $\tilde{z}_x$. For wages *below* a given ceiling, the contributions constitute a variable labour cost, which may be expressed:

$$w_n = \beta(w_s + w_p) = \beta w_s(1 + \alpha) \quad 0 \leq \beta < 1 \tag{5.8}$$

where β is the average social welfare contribution rate on wages. Further, within the relevant region, we do not allow changes in w_s and w_p to involve crossing a wage ceiling and, thus, disrupting the initial allocation as between $\tilde{z}_x$ and w_n. None of these assumptions concerning social welfare can be deemed to be serious if it is recalled that in most OECD countries wage ceilings are set so high that, for the vast majority of workers, the firm's contributions are effectively modelled by expression (5.8). The consequences of ceiling-level changes are discussed, however, in later chapters (particularly Chapters 8 and 9).

No attempt is made to model the possibility of 'backward shifting'; that is, the possibility that increases in β may be offset by reductions in w_s, w_p and w_n. While this would serve to modify outcomes, it is not considered to be of crucial concern for reasons stated in section 4.5.[1]

Given the labour services function (5.2), which distinguishes between workers and hours, we identify, following Hart and Robb (1983), hourly operating costs, s, which vary *only* with the average hours worked per worker. For example, if the firm wishes to extend the work week, then it must incur the extra cost of maintaining an adequate working environment. Obvious cost items here are lighting and heating, but a whole range of other activities, such as security services and canteen facilities, might also be included. These costs are treated as being wholly exogenous.

As for the user cost of capital goods, c, we adopt the standard expression, thus:

$$c = p_k(\delta + \pi) \tag{5.9}$$

where p_k is the price of capital goods, δ is the rate of depreciation and π is the cost of capital.

To round off the model, and following the discussion in section 4.1, we recognise the productivity-enhancing nature of endogenous NWLCs by specifying I in (5.2) as:

$$I = I(z_e/p) \quad I' > 0, I'' < 0 \tag{5.10}$$

where z_e is deflated by a general price index, p, in order to represent the real resource cost. Strictly, z_e in (5.10) should be adjusted by the quit rate since changes in 'once-over' elements (see (5.5)) may partially reflect changes in turnover rates. This possibility is ignored, however.

Using expressions (5.3)–(5.9) and recalling hourly operating costs, s, the firm's total cost function, C, is expressed:

$$C = (\tilde{z}_e + \tilde{z}_x)N + (q + r)(\bar{z}_e + \bar{z}_x)N + w_s(1 + \beta)Nh_s$$
$$+ \alpha w_s(1 + \beta)N(h - h_s) + sh + cK. \qquad (5.11)$$

Such costs are minimised subject to the production constraint, given by combining (5.1), (5.2) and (5.10):

$$Q = \mathrm{F}[I(z_e/p)\mathrm{G}(N,h),K]. \qquad (5.12)$$

The following sub-models comprise restrictions and, in one case, slight modifications to the general problem of minimising (5.11) subject to (5.12).

5.2 PARTICULAR MODELS

Model 5.1

In order to generate some very simple, although useful, results, we impose four basic restrictions on (5.11) and (5.12). The restrictions are that the firm faces fixed standard hours, a fixed capital stock, zero endogenous fixed labour costs and zero hourly operating costs; that is:

$$h_s = \bar{h}_s \qquad (5.13a)$$

$$K = \bar{K} \qquad (5.13b)$$

$$z_e = \tilde{z}_e = \bar{z}_e = 0 \qquad (5.13c)$$

$$s = 0. \qquad (5.13d)$$

Further, in this 'bare bones' model we are not interested in which elements of exogenous fixed labour costs in (5.5) or variable labour costs in (5.6)–(5.8) produce changes in z_x or v, respectively. Combining these simplifications with the restrictions in (5.13) and substituting into the minimisation problem in (5.11) and (5.12) produces the following equilibrium demand equations (see Appendix for details):

$$N^* = N^*(z_x/v, Q) \quad N_1^* < 0, N_2^* > 0 \qquad (5.14a)$$

$$h^* = h^*(z_x/v) \quad h^{*\prime} > 0 \qquad (5.14b)$$

although, as noted in the Appendix, the equilibrium outcomes with respect to the scale variable, Q, are dependent on not too restrictive assumptions about the precise functional form of (5.12). Unequivocally, however, a rise in the ratio of exogenous fixed to variable labour costs produces a desired substitution of more equilibrium hours per worker, h^* for fewer equilibrium workers, N^*.

The nature of these solutions is illustrated with reference to Figure 5.1. The firm is initially employing the equilibrium combination of manhours, $N_0^* h_0^*$, at point A where the cost curve C_0C_0 with slope[2] $-(vN^2)/C$ is tangential to the isoemployment locus, L_0L_0, with slope $-G_N/G_h$ from (5.2) (there is no productivity index, I, by assumption). Consider now two distinct effects that induce the firm to increase its equilibrium workforce from N_0^* to N_1^*; the same employment change under each effect is assumed purely to simplify the diagrammatic presentation. The first is a pure substitution effect and occurs as the result of a *ceteris paribus* fall in the ratio z_x/v. This

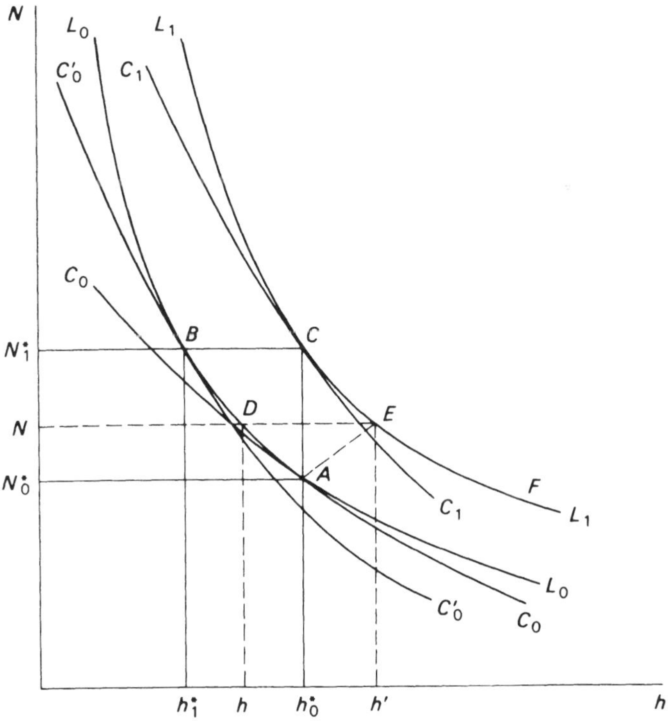

Figure 5.1

induces the firm to increase equilibrium workers and reduce equilibrium hours per worker as shown in Figure 5.1 at point B where the steeper cost curve[3] $C_0'C_0'$ cuts L_0L_0 at $N_1^*h_1^*$ manhours. The second is a scale effect and results from a *ceteris paribus* increase in output, Q, producing a new equilibrium at point C where C_1C_1 cuts L_1L_1. Since equilibrium hours per worker are scale invariant (*given* a suitable functional form of (5.12)), equilibrium manhours are at $N_1^*h_0^*$. Figure 5.1 will prove to be a useful reference for developments in the following two chapters.

We have already indicated that scale outcomes in (5.14a) and (5.14b) depend on the form of the production function in (5.12). Assumptions concerning the production function have a potentially more critical bearing on the outcomes in (5.14a) and (5.14b), however. By far the most popular form of function, for both theoretical and empirical purposes, is the Cobb-Douglas case, which, with respect to Model 5.1, we may write: $Q = dN^{\alpha_1}h^{\alpha_2}$. Now, it is easy to show that if $\alpha_1 < \alpha_2$ then the necessary conditions to achieve a minimum in Model 5.1 do *not* hold. As we shall see in section 6.6(i), the question of the relative sizes of α_1 and α_2 is partly concerned with the issue of non-wage labour costs. It is argued that the evidence tends to support $\alpha_1 > \alpha_2$, the required result in order to proceed here.

Model 5.2

We now relax assumption (5.13a) that standard hours are fixed and we introduce explicitly the various elements of z_x and v. The new equilibrium demand equations are then given by:

$$N^* = N^*(\tilde{z}_x, \bar{z}_x, q, r, h_s, w_s, \alpha, \beta, Q) \tag{5.15a}$$

$$N_i^* < 0 (i = 1, \ldots, 4), N_j^* > 0 (j = 5, \ldots, 8), N_9^* > 0$$

$$h^* = h^*(\tilde{z}_x, \bar{z}_x, q, r, h_s, w_s, \alpha, \beta, Q) \tag{5.15b}$$

$$h_i^* > 0 (i = 1, \ldots, 4), h_j^* < 0 (j = 5, \ldots, 8), h_9^* \geqslant 0$$

where the signs of the partial derivatives are derived in the Appendix. A *ceteris paribus* rise in per-worker costs $(\tilde{z}_x, \bar{z}_x, q, r)$ increases the marginal cost of new employment relative to longer hours worked by existing employees and thus induces substitution of h for N. On the other hand, a *ceteris paribus* rise in standard hours or the standard wage or the overtime premium or the social welfare contribution rate reverses the relative marginal cost increases, thereby encouraging substitution in the opposite direction. The types of equation illustrated in (5.15) have proved to be a popular basis of econometric work and some discussion of empirical findings is made, particularly in relation to worksharing in Chapter 9, at a later stage.

Model 5.3

This model constitutes a variation on Model 5.1 by recognising a specific complication involved in one aspect of US social welfare contributions. In particular, it concerns unemployment insurance, and the model here will prove useful to our discussion of this topic in Chapter 8. As can be seen clearly from Table 2.5, unemployment insurance contribution ceilings in the USA are relatively very low. To all intents and purposes such contributions constitute a fixed labour cost to the firm and thus they should be allocated to $\tilde{z}_x$. There is one complication, however. In the event of an employee changing employers in a given tax year, the tax is non-transferable. This means that if turnover in a given job is such that two, three or more employees hold the job within the tax year then the *full* taxable base (currently standing at $6,000) will apply two, three or more times. Therefore, the higher the turnover rate, the greater the number of jobs with insurance contributions related directly to wages since the higher is the *effective* tax ceiling.

Brechling (1977) has developed the comparative static implications of this particular tax structure for the type of model we are concerned with in this chapter. He describes a total cost function that is formulated in terms of a tax year so that all costs, rates and stocks are expressed in terms of annual averages. Abstracting from the problems of vacations and assuming that annual hours worked are in excess of standard annual hours, a simplified version of Brechling's total cost function can be written:

$$C = \{\tau\tilde{\omega}[1 + q'(1 - \hat{\omega})] + z'_x + v'h\}N \qquad (5.16)$$

where τ is the exogenous payroll tax rate with respect to unemployment insurance, $\tilde{\omega}$ is the taxable wage base, $\hat{\omega}$ is the ratio of the taxable wage base to the actual average variable labour costs (i.e. $\hat{\omega} = \tilde{\omega}/v'h$) and q' is the gross inter-firm labour turnover defined as 'all separations of employees who do not return to the same firm in the same calendar year and who must be replaced by the firm'. Further, z'_x and v' refer to the annual average fixed and variable labour costs excluding unemployment insurance contributions and h and N are also in terms of annual averages.

Consider the problem of minimising (5.16) with respect to the production function of Model 5.1. The simplest insights into the solutions are obtained by reference to the derivations in Model 5.1. Consider the following two restrictions on (5.16):

$$q' = 0 \rightarrow C = (\tau\tilde{\omega} + z_x')N + v'hN \tag{5.17}$$

$$\tilde{\omega} = v'h \rightarrow C = v'hN(\tau + 1) + z_x'N. \tag{5.18}$$

The cost functions in (5.17) and (5.18) exhibit no essential differences from the structure of the cost function in Model 5.1. In (5.17), $q' = 0$ clearly implies that a change in the tax rate, τ, or the wage base, $\tilde{\omega}$, has the same effect as changing z_x in Model 5.1. Thus $\partial N/\partial\tau$, $\partial N/\partial\tilde{\omega} < 0$ and $\partial h/\partial\tau$, $\partial h/\partial\tilde{\omega} > 0$. In (5.18), $\tilde{\omega} = v'h$ (or $\hat{\omega} = 1$) implies that a change in τ has the same effect as a change in v in Model 5.1. Thus $\partial N/\partial\tau > 0$ and $\partial h/\partial\tau < 0$. In the first instance, zero turnover makes the payroll tax a purely fixed cost given that ceiling levels are well below average wages, while, in the second instance, the tax is purely variable since, effectively, the ceiling is completely removed.

It follows quite clearly that, in the absence of the extreme assumptions that produce (5.17) and (5.18), the effects of changes in τ and $\tilde{\omega}$ on N and h cannot be unambiguously signed. The sign of each partial derivative depends on whether or not the per-worker part of the tax predominates over the per-manhour part. Ambiguities also occur for changes in q' and v', although changes in z_x' retain unambiguous implications for workers – hours substitution.

Model 5.4

Restriction (5.13b) is now relaxed, allowing the capital stock to vary. In order to simplify the analysis, but without losing any key results, we retain all the remaining restrictions and simplifications of Model 5.1. As shown in the Appendix, incorporating these changes in the general problem set out in (5.11) and (5.12) produces the following partial derivatives:

$$\begin{aligned} &\partial N^*/\partial z_x < 0 \\ &\partial h^*/\partial z_x \gtrless 0 \\ &\partial K^*/\partial z_x \gtrless 0 \end{aligned} \tag{5.19}$$

$$\begin{aligned} \partial N^*/\partial v &= N(\partial h^*/\partial z_x) + h(\partial N^*/\partial z_x) \lesseqgtr 0 \\ \partial h^*/\partial v &= h(\partial h^*/\partial z_x) + \text{other terms} \lesseqgtr 0 \\ \partial K^*/\partial v &= h(\partial K^*/\partial z_x) + N(\partial h^*/\partial c) \lesseqgtr 0 \end{aligned} \tag{5.20}$$

$$\partial N^*/\partial c \gtreqless 0$$
$$\partial h^*/\partial c \gtreqless 0 \qquad (5.21)$$
$$\partial K^*/\partial c \gtreqless 0.$$

Only one result may be unambiguously signed; as in the previous models, a rise in exogenous fixed labour costs reduces employment. However, as indicated in (5.19), the introduction of a third factor of production precludes the determination of the effect of employment substitution on the other two factors. Here, the signs depend essentially on whether N, h and K act as complements to or substitutes for one another. None of the factor input effects of changes in variable costs in (5.20) can be signed without further restrictions. In Models 5.1 and 5.2, with the capital stock held fixed, an increase in v produces a straightforward worker-for-hours substitution since, in effect, v is rising relative to z_x, which reduces the relative price of the quasi-fixed factor (N) relative to the variable factor (h). Here a rise in v alters the cost structure not only of workers relative to hours per worker but also of manhours relative to capital. Again, knowledge of factor complementarity and substitutionability is needed in order to ascertain actual outcomes. Following the same arguments, the factor input effects of a change in the price of capital goods, c, cannot be signed in (5.21). Further references to this model will be made at a later stage in the text.

Model 5.5

Restrictions (5.13c) and (5.13d) are now relaxed, thereby allowing an element of endogeneity in fixed labour costs to influence labour productivity as well as recognising costs to the firm that vary only with changes in average hours. For simplicity, the stock of capital is fixed; that is, restriction (5.13b) is reimposed. We also retain the working hours restriction and other simplications of Model 5.1. This particular model has been theoretically developed and empirically tested by Hart and Robb (1983). As shown in the Appendix, changes in exogenous fixed costs (z_x) and hourly operating costs (s) produce the only two instances of unambiguous effects on factor inputs. Thus, we obtain:

$$\partial N^*/\partial z_x < 0$$
$$\partial h^*/\partial s < 0. \qquad (5.22)$$

The fall in h for a rise in s occurs for completely analogous economic reasons to the fall in N for a rise in z_x. All remaining partial derivatives with respect to z_x and v are ambiguous. This is the same finding as in the previous sub-model where the capital stock is allowed to vary, and, of course, the underlying economic reasons are essentially the same in the two cases. For example, the firm may react to a fall in N due to an increase in z_x by increasing h *and/or* increasing worker productivity by an increased real expenditure on training, fringe benefits, etc; that is, by increasing z_e/p in (5.12). Again, final outcomes depend on the degree of complementarity and substitutionability among factor inputs that, in the present model, include a qualitative or productivity-based dimension.

5.3 SKILL DISAGGREGATION

Evidence is presented in Table 2.9 and a rationale in section 4.1 to support the possibility that fixed non-wage labour costs are positively related to skill level. With future developments in mind, it is worth noting here a few comparative static results. This is undertaken with the aid of two specific examples.

In the first example, taken from Rosen (1968, pp. 512–13, where precise derivations can be found), advantage is made of the inherent simplicity of Model 5.1 and the modification is introduced that the firm's labour input is divided into two distinct homogeneous groups, $L_1 = G(N_1, h_1)$ and $L_2 = G(N_2, h_2)$. The division occurs because, by assumption, L_2 is a higher-skill group than L_1 with a higher associated per-unit fixed labour cost (training and hiring costs, fringes, etc.). Suppose further that L_1's partial elasticity of substitution with fixed capital stock, $\sigma_{1\bar{K}}$, is greater than L_2', $\sigma_{2\bar{K}}$. Under these conditions, how would an unanticipated fall in output, say, affect the firm's mix of L_1 and L_2 ? The position is illustrated in Figure 5.2. Starting in long-run equilibrium at point A on the isoemployment locus at Q units of output, the firm experiences a decrease in output to Q'. Ignoring for the moment the fixed-cost differences, the new equilibrium is at A′, which represents an increase in the ratio L_2/L_1. The assumption $\sigma_{1\bar{K}} > \sigma_{2\bar{K}}$ provides a sufficient condition for the locus's slope to decrease, moving out along any ray from the origin. The unit fixed-cost inequality implies that the new short-run equilibrium position is to the left of A′, at A″. This occurs because parts of the interest components of fixed costs (see (5.5)) become sunk costs and so the marginal cost of L_2 lowers relative to L_1. The slope at the tangent of the constant cost curve and the isoemployment locus, at A″, is smaller than the previous two equilibrium positions. In summary, the movement A–A′ represents a 'capital effect' and the movement A′–A″ is a 'fixed labour cost effect'. In this example, both effects complement one another, producing a larger ratio L_2/L_1. Of course, if the relative

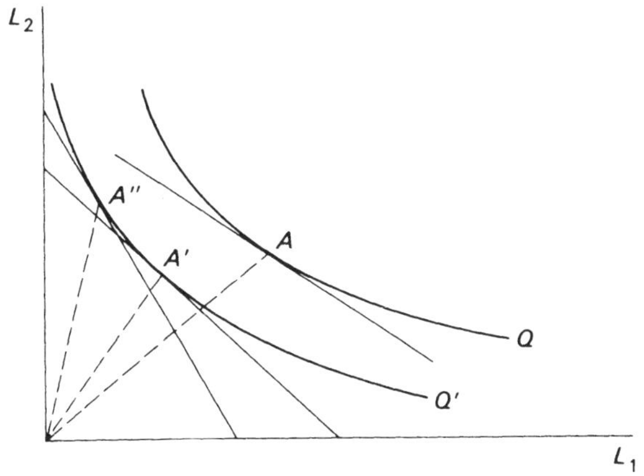

Figure 5.2

sizes of the partial elasticities of substitution were in the opposite direction ($\sigma_{1\bar{K}} < \sigma_{2\bar{K}}$), then the fall in output could produce a ratio L_2/L_1 that is greater than, equal to, or less than the initial equilibrium; this would depend on the relative strengths of the capital substitution and the fixed labour cost effects.

The same skill divisions are used in the second example, but now within the context of Model 5.4. As a special case of (5.12), we assume the operation of a Cobb-Douglas production function. We also generalise expression (5.7) by representing the effect of overtime premium increases on variable costs given longer hours per worker as $\epsilon = (h/v)(\mathrm{d}v/\mathrm{d}h) > 0$. The cost-minimising problem takes the form:

$$\min L(N_i,h_i,K,\lambda) = z_{xi}N_i + v_iN_ih_i + cK$$
$$-\lambda(Q - AN_1^{\alpha_1}h_1^{\alpha_2}K^{\alpha_3}N_2^{\alpha_4}h_2^{\alpha_5})(i = 1, 2). \qquad (5.23)$$

The first-order conditions are given by:

$$L_{N_i} = z_{xi} + v_ih_i - \lambda\alpha_j(Q/N_i) \qquad = 0 \qquad (5.24a)$$
$$(i = 1, 2;\ j = 1/i = 1; j = 4/i = 2)$$

$$L_{h_i} = v_i(1 + \epsilon_i)N_i - \lambda\alpha_j(Q/h_i) \qquad = 0 \qquad (5.24b)$$
$$(i = 1,2;\ j = 2/i = 1;\ j = 5/i = 2)$$

$$L_K = \qquad c - \lambda\alpha_5(Q/K) = 0 \qquad (5.24c)$$

$$L_\lambda = Q - AN_1^{\alpha_1}h_1^{\alpha_2}K^{\alpha_3}N_2^{\alpha_4}h_2^{\alpha_5} \qquad = 0. \qquad (5.24d)$$

Defining $\varrho = \alpha_1 + \alpha_3 + \alpha_4$ and ignoring constant terms, we obtain from (5.24) the following equilibrium expressions for labour and capital inputs:

$$N_1 = Q^{1/\varrho} z_{x_1}^{-(\alpha_2+\alpha_3+\alpha_4)/\varrho} z_{x2}^{(\alpha_4-\alpha_5)/\varrho} c^{\alpha_3/\varrho} v_1^{\alpha_2/\varrho} v_2^{\alpha_5/\varrho} \tag{5.25a}$$

$$h_1 = (z_{x_1}/v_1)/[(\alpha_1/\alpha_2)(1+\epsilon_1)-1] \tag{5.25b}$$

$$K = Q^{1/\varrho} z_{x1}^{(\alpha_1-\alpha_2)/\varrho} z_{x2}^{(\alpha_4-\alpha_5)/\varrho} c^{-(\alpha_1+\alpha_2)/\varrho} v_1^{\alpha_2/\varrho} v_2^{\alpha_5/\varrho} \tag{5.25c}$$

$$N_2 = Q^{1/\varrho} z_{x1}^{(\alpha_1-\alpha_2)/\varrho} z_{x_2}^{-(\alpha_1+\alpha_3+\alpha_5)/\varrho} c^{\alpha_3/\varrho} v_1^{\alpha_2/\varrho} v_2^{\alpha_5/\varrho} \tag{5.25d}$$

$$h_2 = (z_{x_2}/v_2)/[\alpha_4/\alpha_5(1+\epsilon_2)-1]. \tag{5.25e}$$

A number of features of these results are worth noting:

(i) Equilibrium hours equations (5.25b) and (5.25e) are independent of both output changes and cross-price effects. The Cobb-Douglas function is one of a family of functions that produce scale independence in hours, as postulated in Model 5.1 (see equation (5.14b)).

(ii) An increase in z_{x_1} produces a substitution of h_1 for N_1 and may increase or decrease K and N_2 jointly, depending on the relative sizes of α_1 and α_2. Since, in Section 6.6 (i), we incline to the view that $\alpha_1 > \alpha_2$, then the former outcome is perhaps more likely. Equivalent results hold for an increase in z_{x_2}.

(iii) An increase in v_1 produces a reduction in h_1 and a substitution into both N_1 and N_2. However, the strength of the labour substitution is not clear given that the increased v_1 also induces capital–labour substitution. Equivalent results hold for an increase in v_2.

(iv) An increase in c produces worker–capital substitution, leaving hours per worker unchanged.

5.4 SUMMARY OF MAIN RESULTS

In the absence of careful empirical or theoretical reasoning to support the restrictions imposed on each of the five sub-models, they must all be regarded with extreme caution. It might be argued not only that the comparative static structure of each model is incomplete but also that they abstract totally from either dynamic specification or possible simultaneous interaction with other equations outside this immediate system. However, at least they serve to illustrate certain important salient implications of adding non-wage labour costs to the basic production theory of the firm. The essential results of Models 5.4 and 5.5 are retained in the complete development of the problem set out in (5.11) and (5.12) and so the mathematical background is not shown here. Decreases in z_x and s produce positive effects on the size of the workforce and hours per worker, respectively, while all other factor input responses to factor price changes have uncertain outcomes.

Therefore, the worker substitution effect of changes in z_x is a robust result throughout the models here. Moreover, in Models 5.1 and 5.2, the somewhat appealing result holds that a change in z_x produces a straightforward substitution between N and h. As seen in Models 5.4 and 5.5, however, this result is contingent on the exclusion of a second production factor, either quantitative or qualitative. Further, the same set of restrictions in the same models determines whether or not clear-cut results concerning changes in variable non-wage labour costs are attainable.

APPENDIX

The following sets out the most important details concerning the solutions to Models 5.1, 5.2, 5.4 and 5.5 in the text. The essential results to Models 5.1 and 5.2 can be found in Ehrenberg (1971, esp. pp. 8–10 and 112–15); however, some development is given here. An exhaustive examination of Model 5.3 can be found in Brechling (1977).

Model 5.1

Given the assumptions in (5.13a–d), the Lagrangian function for the minimisation problem in (5.11) and (5.12) can be written:

$$L(N, h, \lambda) = z_x N + vNh + \lambda[Q - G(N,h)] \qquad \text{(A5.1)}$$

where λ is a Lagrangian multiplier. The first-order conditions for (A5.1) are:

$$L_N = z_x + vh - \lambda G_N = 0 \qquad \text{(A5.2)}$$

$$L_h = vN - \lambda G_h = 0 \qquad \text{(A5.3)}$$

$$L_\lambda = Q - G(N, h) = 0. \qquad \text{(A5.4)}$$

The determinant of the bordered Hessian matrix is given by:

$$\Delta = \begin{vmatrix} -\lambda G_{NN}, & v - \lambda G_{Nh}, & -G_N \\ v - \lambda G_{hN}, & -\lambda G_{hh}, & -G_h \\ -G_N, & -G_h, & 0 \end{vmatrix}$$

$$= \lambda\ [G_N^2 G_{hh} + G_h^2 G_{NN} + (2G_h^2 G_N)/N - 2G_N G_h G_{Nh}] \quad \text{(A5.5)}$$

using (A5.3). The second-order condition requires $\Delta < 0$ in (A5.5). Since, from (5.2) and (A5.3), λ is positive, this condition requires the *assumption* that the expression inside the square bracket in (A5.5) is negative. This, in turn, dictates that, in order to satisfy this condition, the isoemployment locus (see Figure 5.1) is strictly convex. Given $\Delta < 0$, the following signs of partial derivatives are obtained:

$$\frac{\partial N^*}{\partial z_x} = \frac{G_h^2}{\Delta} < 0 \quad \text{(A5.6a)}$$

$$\frac{\partial N^*}{\partial v} = \frac{G_h^2 h - G_N G_h N}{\Delta} = \frac{-G_h N z_x}{\Delta} > 0 \quad \text{(A5.6b)}$$

from which it follows, using (5.2) and (A5.4), that:

$$\frac{\partial h^*}{\partial z_x} > 0, \ \frac{\partial h^*}{\partial v} < 0 \quad \text{(A5.6c)}$$

as indicated in (5.14a) and (5.14b). Ehrenberg derives the class of production functions, multiplicatively separable in N and h, that satisfies the scale invariance property, $\partial h^*/\partial Q = 0$, in (5.14b): this can be represented generally by the function, $Q = cN^{\alpha}g(h)$. Within this class, Ehrenberg concentrates on a version in which labour is homogeneous and the marginal contribution to labour services of an additional hour of work by one worker is independent of hours of work by all other workers. This allows the production function to be written, $Q = Ng(h)$, which produces $\partial N^*/\partial Q > 0$, as assumed in (5.14a).

Model 5.2

Clearly this model merely breaks down z_x, v and h in the Lagrangian function (A5.1) into constituent parts as shown in section 5.1. From (5.4) and (5.5), $z_x = \tilde{z}_x + (q + r)\bar{z}_x$ and, further, let $w = w_s(1 + \beta)$. Then, in order to derive the partials shown in (5.15a) and (5.15b), it suffices to derive (A5.6a) and the results:

$$\frac{\partial N^*}{\partial h_s} = w(1-\alpha)\frac{\partial N}{\partial z_x} > 0 \qquad \text{(A5.7a)}$$

$$\frac{\partial N^*}{\partial w} = \frac{-z_x w \alpha^2 N^2}{\Delta\lambda^2} > 0 \qquad \text{(A5.7b)}$$

$$\frac{\partial N^*}{\partial \alpha} = \frac{-\alpha w^2 N^2 (z_x + wh_s)}{\Delta\lambda^2} > 0 \qquad \text{(A5.7c)}$$

so that, again using (5.2) and (A5.4), we obtain:

$$\frac{\partial h^*}{\partial h_s}, \frac{\partial h^*}{\partial w}, \frac{\partial h^*}{\partial \alpha} < 0 \qquad \text{(A5.7d)}$$

Model 5.4

The appropriate Lagrangian function for this model is given by:

$$L(N,h,K,\lambda) = z_x N + vNh + cK + \lambda\ [Q - F\ (N,\ h,\ K)]. \qquad \text{(A5.8)}$$

The first-order conditions for (A5.8) are:

$$L_N = z_x + vh - \lambda F_N = 0 \qquad \text{(A5.9)}$$

$$L_h = vN - \lambda F_h = 0 \qquad \text{(A5.10)}$$

$$L_K = c - \lambda F_K = 0 \qquad \text{(A5.11)}$$

$$L_\lambda = Q - F(N, h, K) = 0. \qquad \text{(A5.12)}$$

The determinant of the bordered Hessian matrix is given by:

$$\Delta = \begin{vmatrix} -\lambda F_{NN}, & v - \lambda F_{NK}, & -\lambda F_{NK}, & -F_N \\ v - \lambda F_{hN}, & -\lambda F_{hh}, & -\lambda F_{hK}, & -F_h \\ -\lambda F_{NK}, & -\lambda F_{hK}, & -\lambda F_{KK}, & -F_K \\ -F_N, & -F_h, & -F_K, & 0 \end{vmatrix} \qquad \text{(A5.13)}$$

and we assume $\Delta < 0$ in (A5.13) in order to satisfy the second-order condition for a minimum. We then obtain, using (5.1):

$$\frac{\partial N^*}{\partial z_x} = \frac{1}{\Delta}(\lambda F_h^2 F_{hK} + \lambda F_h F_K F_{hK} - \lambda F_K^2 F_{hh} - \lambda F_h^2 F_{KK}) < 0 \quad \text{(A5.14a)}$$

$$\frac{\partial h^*}{\partial z_x} = \frac{1}{\Delta}(\lambda F_K^2 F_{Nh} + \lambda F_N F_h F_{KK} - \lambda F_N F_K F_{hK} - \lambda F_h F_K F_{NK} - \nu F_K^2) \lesseqgtr 0 \quad \text{(A5.14b)}$$

$$\frac{\partial K^*}{\partial z_x} = \frac{1}{\Delta}(\lambda F_h^2 F_{NK} + \lambda F_N F_K F_{hh} + \nu F_h F_K - \lambda F_N F_h F_{hK} - \lambda F_h F_K F_{hN}) \gtrless 0 \quad \text{(A5.14c)}$$

and

$$\frac{\partial N^*}{\partial \nu} = N\left(\left(\frac{\partial h^*}{\partial z_x}\right) + h\left(\frac{\partial N^*}{\partial z_x}\right) \gtrless 0 \quad \text{(A5.14d)}$$

$$\frac{\partial h^*}{\partial \nu} = h\left(\frac{\partial h^*}{\partial z_x}\right) + \text{(other terms)} \gtrless 0 \quad \text{(A5.14e)}$$

$$\frac{\partial K^*}{\partial \nu} = h\left(\frac{\partial K^*}{\partial z_x}\right) + N\left(\frac{\partial h^*}{\partial c}\right) \gtrless 0. \quad \text{(A5.15f)}$$

Finally:

$$\frac{\partial N^*}{\partial c} = \frac{1}{\Delta}(\lambda F_h^2 F_{NK} + \lambda F_N F_K F_{hh} - \lambda F_N F_h F_{hK} - \lambda F_h F_K F_{Nh}) \gtrless 0 \quad \text{(A5.15g)}$$

and similar developments produce inconclusive signs to $\partial h^*/\partial c$ and $\partial K^*/\partial c$.

Model 5.5

The Lagrangian function is given by:

$$L(N, h, z_e, \lambda) = (z_e + z_x)N + \nu Nh + sh + \lambda[Q - I(z_e/p)G(N, h)]. \quad \text{(A5.16)}$$

The first-order conditions for (A5.8) are:

$$L_N = z_e + z_x + \nu h - \lambda I G_N = 0 \quad \text{(A5.17a)}$$

$$L_h = \nu N + s - \lambda I G_h = 0 \quad \text{(A5.17b)}$$

$$L_{z_e} = \qquad N - \lambda I'G/p = 0 \qquad \text{(A5.17c)}$$

$$L\lambda = Q - I\,(z_e/p)G(N,h) \qquad = 0. \qquad \text{(A5.17d)}$$

The determinant of the bordered Hessian matrix is given by:

$$\Delta = \begin{vmatrix} -\lambda IG_{NN}, & v - \lambda IG_{Nh}, & -\dfrac{\lambda I'G_N}{p}, & -IG_N \\ v - \lambda IG_{hN}, & -\lambda IG_{hh}, & -\dfrac{\lambda I'G_h}{p}, & -IG_h \\ 1 - \dfrac{\lambda I'G_N}{p}, & -\dfrac{\lambda I'G_h}{p}, & -\dfrac{\lambda I''G}{p}, & -\dfrac{I'G}{p} \\ -IG_N, & -IG_h, & -\dfrac{I'G}{p}, & 0 \end{vmatrix} \qquad \text{(A5.18)}$$

where, again, we assume $\Delta < 0$ in order to satisfy the second-order conditions. Clearly, the structure of this model bears many similarities to Model 5.4. It is easily checked that:

$$\frac{\partial N^*}{\partial z_x} < 0 \qquad \text{(A5.19a)}$$

while

$$\frac{\partial h^*}{\partial z_x}, \frac{\partial z_e^*}{\partial z_x} \gtrless 0. \qquad \text{(A5.19b)}$$

and

$$\frac{\partial h^*}{\partial s} < 0 \qquad \text{(A5.19c)}$$

where

$$\frac{\partial N^*}{\partial s}\left(= \frac{\partial h^*}{\partial z_x}\right), \frac{\partial z_e^*}{\partial s} \gtrless 0. \qquad \text{(A5.19d)}$$

The remaining comparative static results can be written:

$$\frac{\partial N^*}{\partial v} = h\left(\frac{\partial N^*}{\partial z_x}\right) + N\left(\frac{\partial N^*}{\partial s}\right) \gtrless 0 \qquad \text{(A5.19e)}$$

$$\frac{\partial h^*}{\partial v} = h\left(\frac{\partial h^*}{\partial z_x}\right) + N\left(\frac{\partial h^*}{\partial s}\right) \gtrless 0 \qquad \text{(A5.19f)}$$

$$\frac{\partial z_e^*}{\partial v} = h\left(\frac{\partial z_e^*}{\partial z_x}\right) + N\left(\frac{\partial z_e^*}{\partial s}\right) \gtrless 0. \qquad \text{(A5.19g)}$$

NOTES

1 Also, it is assumed that changes in variable costs in (5.6) do not affect quits in (5.5). Models that do accommodate this possibility are discussed in the next chapter.
2 From (5.11), given (5.13), $N = C/(z_x + vh)$ and so, given C, $dN/dh = -vN^2/C$.
3 Using the result in the previous note, and given N and h: $\partial(dN/dh)/\partial z_x = vN^3/C^2 > 0$, i.e. given v, a fall in z_x will algebraically decrease the slope of CC, while $\partial(dN/dh)/\partial v = -z_x N^3/C^2 < 0$, i.e. given z_x, an increase in v will decrease the slope of CC.

REFERENCES

Brechling, F. (1965), 'The relationship between output and employment in British manufacturing industries', *Review of Economic Studies,* 32, 187–216.

Brechling, F. (1977), 'The incentive effects of the US unemployment insurance tax', *Research in Labor Economics,* Vol. 1, Greenwich, Conn.: JAI Press.

Ehrenberg, R. G. (1971), *Fringe Benefits and Overtime Behavior,* Massachusetts: Heath & Co.

Feldstein, M. S. (1967), 'Specification of the labour input in the aggregate production function', *Review of Economic Studies,* 34, 375–386.

Hart, R. A. and A. L. Robb (1983), 'Production and labour demand functions with endogenous fixed worker costs', Berlin: International Institute of Management, mimeo.

Nadiri, M. I. and S. Rosen (1969), 'Interrelated factor demand functions', *American Economic Review,* 59, 457–471.

National Board for Prices and Incomes (1970), *Hours of Work, Overtime and Shiftworking,* Report No. 161, London: HMSO.

Rosen, S. (1968), 'Short-run employment variation on class-I railroads in the US, 1947–1963', *Econometrica,* 36, 511–529.

University College, Galway (1980), *A Study of Overtime Working in Ireland,* Vol I and II, Galway, Ireland: University College for Irish government departments of Labour and of Economic Planning, and Commission of the European Communities.

6 Cyclical Employment Effects

The timeless quality of the comparative static framework seriously limits its usefulness. Indeed, one of the major arguments for the need to introduce a dynamic time perspective into the foregoing models is concerned with the very fact that the models themselves incorporate fixed non-wage labour costs. Given the costs associated with search, hiring and layoff, firms are unlikely to be either willing or able to respond immediately to changing the composition of their manhours in response to factor price changes or expected sales changes. Delays in factor-adjustment response in the face of transactions costs require reconstituting the arguments of Chapter 5 within a time dimension. More importantly for present purposes, attempting to incorporate adjustment lags helps not only to reinforce several important comparative static results but also to extend the usefulness of the analysis. Of particular interest in this latter respect is the fact that the dynamic setting enables strong and testable hypotheses to be advanced concerning cyclical employment and wage behaviour and it is on these aspects of the subject that the present and the next chapters respectively concentrate.

In this chapter, we begin by illustrating the standard approach towards accommodating delayed factor-adjustment response to desired factor input combinations. The basic ideas are conveyed in section 6.1, via a simple extension to Model 5.1, and in section 6.2, which builds on this foundation by introducing capital and its rate of utilisation into the analysis. In section 6.3, we discuss a particular model that also deals with dynamic factor-adjustment response given fixed NWLCs but without reliance on the modelling assumption that adjustment takes place with respect to a set of static equilibrium points. The model lays great emphasis on involuntary layoffs as a mechanism by which the firm adjusts its workforce to cyclical falls in demand. An alternative model is then reviewed in section 6.4, which, in somewhat sharp contrast, gives a central role to voluntary quits and layoffs as determinants of the size of the workforce. Despite their differences in approach, all the models produce reasonably similar expectations as to the cyclical behaviour of the labour input and, accordingly, we examine some relevant empirical evidence in section 6.5. Two related areas of labour market interest, with strong grounding in the research developments in this area, are discussed in section 6.6; these are the size of the returns to labour services in production function analysis and the so-called reserve labour hypothesis. Finally, section 6.7 deals briefly with related work on the analysis of labour markets disaggregated by geographical regions.

6.1 A SIMPLE ILLUSTRATION

Consider the simplest of the comparative static models, Model 5.1 and, in particular, its equilibrium solutions given in (5.14). Suppose that the firm's initial equilibrium manhours mix is at point A in Figure 5.1, corresponding to N_0^* employees working average hours, h_0^*. As before, a *ceteris paribus* fall in the ratio z_x/v induces a desired substitution to the new mix N_1^*, h_1^*. The restriction is now imposed that, given search, training and other adjustment costs, the firm cannot fill the employment gap $N_1^* - N_0^*$ in a given finite period. Instead, at the end of the period it employs $N - N_0^*$ new employees where $N < N_1^*$. Note that Model 5.1 assumes that there are no equivalent fixed costs associated with changing hours of work.[1] In this model, it is assumed that hours play a passive or accommodating role of ensuring that, for any given N, the firm can meet its labour services requirement. In this present example, as long as the actual workforce lies below its desired level, actual hours lie above equilibrium hours as compensation so as to remain on the isoemployment locus L_0L_0. On the other hand, a rise in z_x/v will reverse these outcomes. Here, the desired workforce will fall but the actual workforce may exhibit an adjustment lag as firms seek to spread their adjustment costs, such as redundancy payments, over some finite time horizon. Again, assuming no equivalent costs of adjusting hours, actual hours will lie below desired hours to compensate a surfeit of the actual over the desired workforce.

Returning to the initial equilibrium at A, suppose there is a desired increase in labour services requirement to L_1L_1 given a *ceteris paribus* permanent output increase. The new desired equilibrium position is at point C, with an N_1^*, h_0^* manhours combination. In this case, the transactions costs associated with fixed labour investments prevent the firm from taking its optimum expansion path, A–C. Again, in a given finite period, it can only achieve $N - N_0^*$ labour force expansion thereby constraining its route to the new isoemployment locus to be A–E. Actual hours per worker are expanded beyond their long-run scale equilibrium position, to h', in order to compensate the shortfall in the desired workforce size. Assuming no further output shocks to the model, adjustment to equilibrium then takes place as in the previous case.

Introducing time explicitly into the discussion and letting $N_t^*(h_t^*)$ and $N_t(h_t)$ be the respective desired and actual levels of workers (hours per worker) at time t, we have, combining Model 5.1's version of (5.2) with (5.14):

$$L_t = g(N_t^*, h_t^*) = g(N_t, h_t) = f[(z_x/v)_t, Q_t]. \tag{6.1}$$

Changes in $(z_x/v)_t$ and/or Q_t, following the above two examples, imply that substitution between workers and hours takes the form:

$$(h_t^* - h_t) = -\gamma(N_t^* - N_t). \tag{6.2}$$

Thus, for example, a short-term excess supply of labour ($N_t^* < N_t$) is compensated by a shortfall in actual, as compared to desired, hours ($h_t^* > h_t$). We round off this simple system by representing the partial adjustment of N_t to N_t^* in a given finite period by the stock adjustment process:

$$N_t - N_{t-1} = \lambda(N_t^* - N_{t-1}) \quad 0 < \lambda < 1. \tag{6.3}$$

Again recalling that hours are assumed to be purely variable in this model, the solutions to (6.1), (6.2) and (6.3) yield the following recursive labour demand functions:

$$N_t = N_t[(z_x/v)_t, Q_t, N_{t-1}] \tag{6.4a}$$

$$h_t = h_t[(z_x/v)_t, Q_t, N_{t-1}]. \tag{6.4b}$$

This, essentially, comprises the simple system developed and tested by Hart and Sharot (1978), Kirwan (1979) and Bell (1981).

6.2 INTERRELATED FACTOR DEMAND MODELS

The system depicted in (6.4) is essentially a special case of a general structure originally developed in a series of seminal publications by Nadiri and Rosen (1969; 1974a, b). They generalise beyond (6.4) in two major directions. First, they allow for the dichotomy between stocks and utilisation rates in the capital as well as the labour input. Just as fixed worker costs may serve to produce a relatively rapid short-run response in labour utilisation given changes in factor prices and/or demand, so fixed capital costs (see expression (5.9)) may produce a similar relative response in capacity utilisation rates (c_u). Second, they treat the input adjustment costs as a fully interrelated system; disequilibrium in any one input can influence the adjustment responses of the other three.

The incorporation of interrelated factor demands into their system is effected by a generalisation of the stock adjustment model as represented by (6.3); thus;

$$Y_{jt} - Y_{jt-1} = (\beta_{ij})(Y^*_{it} - Y_{it-1})(j = 1, \ldots, 4) \tag{6.4}$$

where Y is a 4×1 vector of factor inputs ($i = N, h, K$ and c_u, respectively) and β_{ij} is a 4×4 matrix of adjustment coefficients, with $1 \leq \beta_{ij} \leq 0$. Given this additional overlay, their methodology proceeds in the same way as in Model 5.4, with the additional modification that c_u enters the model by functionally relating it to capital stock depreciation (δ in (5.9)). Therefore, as in Model 5.4, desired factor inputs are implicitly related to factor prices and output and so (6.4) may be written in the form:

$$Y_{it} - Y_{it-1} = \sum_{j=1}^{4} \beta_{ij}[G_j(z_{xt}, v_t, c_t, Q_t) - Y_{jt-1}] \quad (i = 1, \ldots, 4). \tag{6.5}$$

It is useful to the discussion to rewrite (6.5) more fully; using the lag operator, L (i.e. $LY_{it} = Y_{it-1}$, etc.) and rearranging, it can be written as:

$$\begin{bmatrix} 1-(1-\beta_{11})L & \beta_{12}L & \beta_{13}L & \beta_{14}L \\ \beta_{21}L & 1-(1-\beta_{22})L & \beta_{23}L & \beta_{24}L \\ \beta_{31}L & \beta_{32}L & 1-(1-\beta_{33})L & \beta_{34}L \\ \beta_{41}L & \beta_{42}L & \beta_{43}L & 1-(1-\beta_{44})L \end{bmatrix} \begin{bmatrix} Y_{1t} \\ Y_{2t} \\ Y_{3t} \\ Y_{4t} \end{bmatrix} = \begin{bmatrix} \beta_{11} & \beta_{12} & \beta_{13} & \beta_{14} \\ \beta_{21} & \beta_{22} & \beta_{23} & \beta_{24} \\ \beta_{31} & \beta_{32} & \beta_{33} & \beta_{34} \\ \beta_{41} & \beta_{42} & \beta_{43} & \beta_{44} \end{bmatrix} \begin{bmatrix} G_1() \\ G_2() \\ G_3() \\ G_4() \end{bmatrix} \tag{6.6}$$

In the absence of strong *a priori* assumptions, the usual rationale for the model structure in (6.6) runs as follows. Each factor input has an expected short-run adjustment cost. Higher expected values of costs will be positively correlated with the degree of fixity of each input factor. Inputs with relatively low adjustment costs will be adjusted to product demand and factor price changes relatively speedily, thus exhibiting relatively large β_{ij}'s. This helps to achieve a given labour and capital services requirement as quickly as possible through compensation for relatively high-cost inputs, which, partly owing to higher associated financial risks, are adjusted relatively slowly. Nadiri and Rosen and subsequent writers argue that the 'stock' variables, workers and capital, will be expected to adjust more slowly than their respective 'flow' variables, hours per worker and capacity utilisation (i.e. $\beta_{22} > \beta_{11}, \beta_{44} > \beta_{33}$). Moreover if, as in the previous model, both h_t and c_{ut} act as variable factors of production and serve to fill in the gaps between desired and actual stock levels, then we would expect $\beta_{22} = \beta_{44} = 1.0$ and $\beta_{21}, \beta_{43} > 0$. However, at least with respect to the labour input, a number of factors conspire to leave the size of the relative adjustment speeds as an open empirical question. For example, we have already noted in our general model framework, and in Model 5.5, that there are fixed costs associated with changing hours per worker. Additionally, Hart and McGregor (1982) suggest further fixity elements associated with changing average hours. In section 6.5 below, empirical evidence is discussed concerning the sizes of own- and cross-adjustment parameters in (6.6).

6.3 NICKELL'S FIXED COST MODEL

While the overlay of a constrained adjustment process enriches the simple static models of Chapter 5, there remains a distinct air of unreality over the manner in which the actual adjustment takes place. Given expectations concerning relative factor prices and output, firms are assumed to perceive, at any point in time, some static equilibrium point towards which they optimally adjust factor inputs subject to a set of adjustment constraints. Information costs and uncertainty may well be such that the firm's actual adjustment response is better conditioned by a simpler, and possibly cheaper, set of rules. For example, it may expect some pattern of cyclical variation in product demand and seek to maximise profits or minimise costs by choosing an optimal adjustment path of factor inputs that are consistent with this pattern as well as its normal production constraints. Nickell (1978) sets out to study the demand for labour in the presence of fixed hiring and firing costs given such a structure. In his model, the firm operates M_t machines at time, t, for h_t hours per week. The firm has a fixed stock of machines, M^*. There is one worker per machine who also works h_t hours. As for non-wages, attention is concentrated on the fixed, non-recurrent costs associated with changing the labour stock; rates of A_t accessions and D_t discharges incur per-worker costs of a and d, respectively. Recurring fixed and variable non-wage labour costs are subsumed into a general expression, $W(h)$, which represents weekly employment costs. However, weekly fixed costs as well as guaranteed 'fall-back' pay during slack periods are also important to the arguments since they serve to prevent weekly hours from falling back far enough to induce voluntary quits, which are excluded from the model. A regular, fully anticipated, demand cycle requires x_t units of output per week, which is produced by hM machine-hours (equal to manhours). Given a fixed output price, p, and discount rate, r, the profit-maximising firm confronts the problem:

$$\max \int_0^{\infty} e^{-rt}[phM - W(h)M - aA - dD]\,dt \tag{6.7}$$

subject to five constraints. The first follows from the assumptions of no inventories and no production in excess of demand; i.e.:

$$x_t - h_t M_t \geq 0. \tag{6.8a}$$

The remaining four are self-explanatory, i.e.:

$$M^* - M_t \geq 0 \tag{6.8b}$$

$$\dot{M} = A_t - D_t \tag{6.8c}$$

$$A \geq 0 \tag{6.8d}$$

$$D \geq 0. \tag{6.8e}$$

The general solution to this variational problem is analysed by Nickell in terms of critical stages in the demand cycle. In periods of excess demand ($x_t - h_t M_t > 0$ in (6.8a)), in the neighbourhood of cyclical output demand peaks, the full stock of machines, M^*, are worked for fixed weekly hours, h^*, where h^* satisfies the condition that the marginal costs of hours ($W'(h^*)$) equals fixed output price, p. As demand slackens, the next phase is reached whereby excess demand is cleared ($x_t = hM_t$) and hours fall as a function of falling demand with no change in the number of machines in operation. In both these phases, $M^* = M$ ensures that $A = D = 0$ in (6.8d) and (6.8e). The following phase, which precedes the trough of the cycle marks a switch in the roles of dismissals and hours. The latter are fixed[2] and the number of machines in operation falls with falling output demand. Now $M^* - M_t > 0$ in (6.8b) and $D > 0$ in (6.8e). The trough, or 'slump phase', of the cycle is marked by a constant number of machines in operation with, once again, changes in hours accommodating changes in demand. The upturn of the cycle to excess demand 'mirrors' the downturn, with accessions, A, replacing the role of dismissals, D.

Thus, for the individual firm, the model predicts lagged hours and employment responses to output changes, with the special feature that each phase marks a change in hours *or* employment (or neither). Aggregating over diverse firms to industry level, or industries to economy level, is likely to produce a set of labour reactions that are very similar to Nadiri and Rosen's *a priori* expectations. In terms of distributed lag responses, a change in output from a cyclical peak or trough will produce a lag function in hours with a high proportion of weights concentrated in the early periods of the distribution[3] with employment weights either more evenly distributed over a larger number of initial periods or with a 'humped' appearance following a delayed response.

Finally, among several other interesting features, two useful predictions concerning the effects of NWLC changes on labour hoarding are gained from the model. First, for a given demand cycle, an increase in hiring and/or firing costs (a and d in (6.7)) will induce the firm to reduce its stock of machines and utilise a higher proportion of the stock during the slump phase. Accordingly, labour hoarding will be increased, with more workers employed for fewer hours. Second, an increase in recurring fixed non-wages (which are explicitly introduced into the $W(h)$ expression) reduces *both* the stock of machines *and* the number operated during the slump, thereby reducing labour hoarding and increasing hours per worker.

6.4 OKUN'S TOLL MODEL

More recently, Okun (1981) has developed an analysis of the cyclical consequences of fixed non-recurring NWLCs as one of the central features of a general macroeconomic system. Developing a standard search model of the labour market, he considers the consequences to the firm of paying, at the point of hiring, a substantial non-recurrent 'toll' on each new worker. While the essentials of the analysis proceed 'as if' the toll constitutes a crude employment head tax imposed exogenously by the government, its specific make-up comprises the screening, training and other costs introduced in section 4.1. The toll is interpreted by Okun as a form of set-up cost that, by mutual agreement, is shared between the employer and the worker in such a way as to establish the conditions under which their future relationship can evolve. In its essential features the toll model fleshes out the economic analyses and arguments to be found in Oi (1962) and, especially, Salop (1973).

For simplicity, workers are treated as homogeneous. However, the existence of the toll makes it important to distinguish between new recruits and established workers. In strict parallel to the decision constraint developed by Oi (see expression (4.5)), the firm will pay both new recruits and established workers a wage that, at any point in time, lies below their marginal value product. The net return to the firm will depend on the amount of the initial toll relative to the size of the gap between the wage and the marginal value product (discounted each time-period) times the length of the worker's life with the firm.

The firm is likely to endeavour to shift at least a part of the toll cost on to new recruits. The most likely way to achieve this is to pay a lower wage over some initial period while at the same time offering an incentive to the recruit to accept this state of affairs. For example, both sides may enter into an explicit time contract, which covers a period that allows them to have a reasonable chance of recouping their respective shares of the toll investment. Alternatively, given potential problems of inflexibility and moral hazard entailed with such a contract, a more implicit agreement may be more suitable to both sides. Firms can reinforce the chances of desired outcomes by adopting discriminatory hiring policies that involve screening for the 'type' of worker likely to prefer long job tenure. It can also offer fringe benefits, the returns to which are positively related to length of tenure. For their part, intending new workers can seek information from established workers concerning the firm's credibility *vis-à-vis* both the length of payment of the initial wage and the potential for the second-tier wage path. At any point in time, this latter wage will lie between the marginal value product of established workers and their opportunity wage or the wage earned if they were new recruits elsewhere. The position of the wage within this range establishes the degree to which employer and worker share the quasi-rent from the toll investment.

Since all elements of the toll are non-recurring fixed NWLCs (and thus equivalent to $\bar{z}$ in expression (5.5)), they vary directly with the quit rate. Following the approach of Salop (1973) (see also Pencavel, 1972), Okun adds an overlay to the foregoing structure by postulating that the quit rate is a negative function of the wage.[4] Higher wages reduce quits and thereby lengthen the average period over which the toll investment is discounted. The firm will seek to choose the combination of wages and (expected) quits that minimises total labour costs or maximises profits. Wages that satisfy these optimising conditions are likely to be chosen from the dual wage system, which gives a premium for seniority, rather than one unified wage. The main reason for this is as follows. Workers who are most likely to accept a lower initial wage with a prospect of a higher wage later are likely to be those who will wish to remain with the firm for a period that allows them, at least, to recover their share of the initial investment. In this event the firm will be encouraged to choose the optimum wage/quit combination from a self-selected group that exhibits relatively low *a priori* quit probabilities. Of course, this still leaves the choice of the optimal dual wage combination, which, among other factors, will be a function of the degree of workers' risk aversion and their time preferences.

In an implicit contract under this dual wage structure, the main signal from the firm to a worker concerning its long-term employment intentions is its willingness to make the toll investment. Workers for their part signal intentions of long job tenure by accepting the initial lower wage. A complication to this state of affairs will arise if the firm experiences an unexpected fall in output demand. Particularly serious in this respect would be a fall in demand for the firm's own product that is proportionately greater than for those of its competitors. If the firm reacts by cutting wages or, more likely, by indicating that wages will grow below their previously anticipated path, it runs the risk of provoking an unprecedented number of quits of both new recruits and established workers. Average job lengths would fall and per-period toll costs to the firm, the periodic rent in Oi's terminology, would rise. Anticipation of such repercussions may well lead the firm to limit or even reject a wage response. Reluctance to change wages will vary inversely with the expected length of the demand fall. The shorter this expectation then the more sustainable will be the drop in the marginal value product relative to the wage. Even a general demand fall, affecting competing firms in a similar manner, may well produce comparable reactions in the firm's wage policy. The firm will be unsure of the wage responses of its competitors and, therefore, of the degree of the potential quit-threat it faces. For example, if the firm incorrectly anticipates a longer period of demand downturn than some of its competitors, and cuts its wage more than proportionately to them, it may well experience substantial quits in the subsequent recovery period as its workers perceive a greater default on implicit contractual commitments than elsewhere.

In times of a demand fall, the firm will pay a wage above marginal value product so long as its calculations suggest that the discounted costs of this action are less than the discounted costs of increased toll payments (following a strategy of wage cut/higher quits) that it will incur when demand is restored. This action will tend to dry up quits during the fall-off in demand compared to their flow during normal periods. The toll model fits well, therefore, with the generally observed feature that quit rates are pro-cyclical. A corollary to a reduction in quit rates during the demand fall is an increase in labour hoarding. In the absence of a build-up in inventories in exact compensation to the shortfall in output demand, hoarding is likely to manifest itself in the observation of pro-cyclical changes in labour productivity. Again, this is a well-observed empirical phenomenon but one that is no less consistent with the foregoing models. The toll model also has strong cyclical implications for layoffs and short-time working, issues that are returned to in Chapter 8.

Recently, Gordon (1982) has criticised Okun's book for its over-commitment to an explanation of why wages would be expected to be sticky. While the thrust of Gordon's objections stems from empirical macro observations of wage (and price) changes over long historical time-series in several countries, a similar criticism may also be raised at the micro level. An essential feature of Okun's analysis is that it is in the interest of both the firm and the workforce, through an explicit or implicit contact, to share the quasi-rents that accrue to toll investments. In this event, as we shall see in the next chapter, there may arise a great incentive for both sides to agree to cuts in wages during demand falls. It may well be the case that, given a sharing agreement, the more significant the toll investment, the greater the potential wage cutback for any given demand fall.

6.5 SOME EMPIRICAL FINDINGS ON CYCLICAL EMPLOYMENT–HOURS RESPONSES

All the models discussed in this chapter concentrate on the cyclical adjustment of the labour input given fixed non-wage labour costs associated with the size of the workforce. Explicitly or implicitly it is assumed that there are no, or insignificant, fixed NWLCs related to changes in hours per worker. The theories all predict that short-term employment variations that accompany demand changes will be smaller the greater the degree of labour fixity. As a corollary, given lower unit fixed costs of changing hours, Rosen (1968) and Nadiri and Rosen (1969) postulate that hours' variation should be higher the greater the degree of labour fixity. Moreover, as emphasised by Oi and Rosen, and illustrated in the discussion concerning Figure 5.2, these results will be reinforced if the degree of labour fixity is negatively correlated with the degree of substitutionability with the fixed capital factor. Such an outcome may be expected, for example, under the condition that the bulk of labour investments paid for by the firm are relatively firm-specific.

On the assumption that fixed labour costs are positively correlated with the level of skill, Rosen tested the employment variation hypothesis using data describing different skill groups of employees on US class-I railroads between 1947 and 1963. He found that the rankings of relative employment variation and, with one exception, relative hours' variation[5] to be in the expected direction. Further estimates of long-run factor substitution parameters, using cross-sectional data for twenty-seven class-I railroads in 1959 and 1960, indicated strongly that high fixed-cost labour inputs were worse substitutes for fixed short-run factors than low fixed-cost inputs. Thus the predictions of employment variability given fixed costs would seem to be reinforced, on this evidence, by the substitution hypothesis. For his test of the employment variation hypothesis, Oi assumed that occupational wage differences proxy differences in the degree of labour fixity. He then used a χ^2 contingency table test for selected industries to test the null hypothesis that no relationship exists between wage rates and the observed rate of change of employment. The data rejected the hypothesis in favour of the alternative hypothesis that high-wage occupations experience relatively lower employment changes: again, these results support the employment variation hypothesis. As a simple forerunner to the interdependent systems of Nadiri and Rosen, Oi found that, for the years 1920–39, the short-run adjustment lag in a simple partial-adjustment employment model was significantly larger for production as compared with non-production workers. As mentioned in section 4.3 in relation to Soligo (1966), non-production workers would be expected to possess higher per capita fixed investments than production workers.

In the simple illustration in section 6.1, a once-for-all unanticipated permanent rise in output produces a relatively large short-run response in hours per worker that offsets a relatively small employment response given associated fixed adjustment costs. Gradually, and in the absence of other output shocks, manhours equilibrium is restored by the substitution of workers for hours. Generalising somewhat, it might be expected that the high hours/low employment response would characterise the firm's early reactions to permanent output changes. Given an output rise, it will initially be uncertain whether or not it should incur the fixed investments associated with recruitment, etc. As more time elapses, the firm will grow to realise that the change is permanent, thereby increasing its workforce and reducing hours per worker. Comparably, it will initially hesitate over incurring significant firing costs given a fall in output thus producing a similar downward relative response in hours and employment. These responses are implied not only in Nadiri and Rosen's *a priori* economic reasoning but also in Nickell's more formal modelling.

This implies a lead-time in the turning points of hours per worker as compared to corresponding employment, with the length of lead positively correlated with the degree of labour fixity. Further, if output increases affect different occupations contemporaneously then the employment of relatively high fixed-cost workers should lag that of relatively low fixed-cost workers, while hours per worker among the former should lead those among the latter. An examination of the dates of specific cycle turning points by occupational group in Rosen's railroad study tends generally to validate these expectations. As a more direct test, Rosen fitted distributed lag schemes to monthly data of the workers/hours per worker ratio regressed on manhours as a proxy for output. These showed that the first month's changes in this ratio are due principally to changes in hours per worker followed by a greater employment response in subsequent months. Also, the initial hours' response tended to be greater the higher the fixed-cost occupation. Some, though by no means strong, confirmation of these findings can be found in the reported results of the more general interrelated system of Nadiri and Rosen.

While a few features of Nadiri and Rosen's US findings have proved to be common to similar model estimates derived from other data sets, there is no doubt that significant variations have been found in the relative sizes and strengths of both own- and cross-factor adjustment coefficients. European examples that exhibit quite significant divergences are to be found in Briscoe and Peel (1975) for the UK and Hart and McGregor (1982) for the FRG. One major reason for this may well be due to general specification error. Just as the motivation behind Nickell's model was to move away from the adjustment to static equilibrium approaches, so it has been argued that the fixed-adjustment coefficient system represented by (6.6) should be replaced by models that allow for dynamic adjustment costs consistent with the firm's inter-temporal cost-minimising objectives. While such models have been developed (see Berndt *et al.*, 1979, and McIntosh, 1983), there seems to be little evidence to date of better empirical performance.

Of course, a major reason for divergences may well simply be the existence of different relative adjustment costs between industries and/or countries. For example, at national macro-level, Hart and McGregor (1982) find, for FRG manufacturing industry, relatively speedier worker compared to hours adjustment, which may well indicate the importance of modelling or at least recognising the fixed costs associated with changing average hours. At industry level, Nadiri and Rosen (1974b) obtain results for US durable industries (see their Table 1, p. 266) that indicate a speedier adjustment of production workers than hours per worker while, for non-durable industries (Table 2, p. 267), the two speeds are not statistically different from one another.

6.6 TWO RELATED ISSUES

(i) Returns to Labour Services in Production Functions

Dynamic adjustment apart, the Nadiri and Rosen methodology, in common with the approach adopted in Chapter 5, involves minimising the firm's total cost function subject to a production constraint. Let us assume, in line with most authors, that the production function is adequately modelled by a Cobb-Douglas technical formulation. Ignoring stochastic features as well as time- and cross- section subscripts, we may write the function, in terms of Nadiri and Rosen's system, as:

$$Q = AN^{\alpha_1}h^{\alpha_2}K^{\alpha_3}c_u^{\alpha_2}. \tag{6.9}$$

Many papers have been devoted to estimating the model in (6.9), or restricted versions of it.[6] A common empirical finding is that the labour input exhibits *increasing* returns (i.e. $\alpha_1 + \alpha_2 > 1$) and, for models that separate N and h, this is usually found to be the result of increasing returns to average hours ($0 < \alpha_1 < 1 < \alpha_2$). This has provoked attempts either to rationalise the finding or to show that it is due to some sort of specification error. Elements of both the rationalisation and remodelling approaches involve non-wage labour costs in their arguments.

The best-known examples under the rationalisation heading are provided by Feldstein (1967), who estimates cross-sectional versions of (6.9), and Craine (1973), who estimates a time-series version. Both authors' models exhibit increasing returns to h in their data samples and both explain this result in terms of non-recurring fixed NWLCs. The argument is simple: since some components of such costs, such as set-up time and tea-breaks, tend to concentrate within normal working hours, an extension of working time into premium hours may produce a more than proportionate increase in productive hours. Feldstein offers the additional explanation that increasing h may reduce the per-unit cost of capital services, assuming capital is measured as a stock, because of proportionately lower increases in depreciation and interest charges. If valid, the claim that one should expect, *a priori*, the result $\alpha_1 < \alpha_2$ in (6.9) has serious implications for the approach to modelling adopted in Chapter 5. The necessary condition to achieve minimum solutions to these problems, given a Cobb-Douglas production technology, is that $\alpha_1 > \alpha_2$ (see, for example, Bell, 1982).

The acceptance that, theoretically, one may expect the elasticity of output with respect to hours to be greater than that with respect to workers and, moreover, that there may well be increasing returns to the labour input has been vigorously challenged from a number of directions. Nadiri and Rosen argue, as does Tatom (1980), that it is the exclusion of capacity utilisation from (6.9) that is the main culprit for these results. The seemingly high returns to labour input in fact reflect the returns to both labour *and* capital utilisation. The inclusion of capacity utilisation may help to distinguish between *measured* hours and *effective* hours within the production function (see section 6.6(ii) below). In the event, their results appear strongly to support this view as well as the result that returns to workers are greater than returns to hours. (See, for example, Nadiri and Rosen, 1969, pp. 468–9.)

The main motivation behind the explanation offered by Leslie and Wise (1980) for the observed increasing returns to labour services is an unexplained assertion that the length of average hours is positively correlated with firm efficiency. They allow for this possibility in a pooled cross-section/time-series model that allows for inter-industry variations in efficiency through both scale and slope dummy variables. Prior to the inclusion of both types of dummy variable, they obtain results similar to those obtained by Feldstein ($\alpha_1 < 1$, $\alpha_2 > 1$), while their full specification produces diminishing returns in both N and h and, indeed, supports statistically the hypothesis, $\alpha_1 = \alpha_2$. It is difficult to produce a convincing theoretical argument to support a systematic correlation between firm efficiency and working hours but there is reason, nevertheless, to expect a systematic association between hours of work and type of industry. Given labour's quasi-fixity and acknowledging the high degree of capital fixity, we might expect, at least in the short run, that firms with higher factor fixity will utilise their production factors more intensively in more depressed periods. This result is implied in a number of the models discussed above. Thus, we might anticipate, as suggested in Table 2.9 for the UK, a positive correlation between the degree of factor fixity by industry and the length of working hours. This argument lends general support to the procedure adopted by Leslie and Wise.

Both of these explanations suggest that increasing returns are observed owing to the omission of variables that are key to the modelling of production functions. An explanation along the same lines is suggested by Model 5.5, which allows for an index of worker productivity as an argument in the production function. Given that this index is, in turn, functionally related to endogenous fixed worker costs then, for reasons similar to those supporting Leslie and Wise's approach to modelling, this variable may display a systematic correlation with hours of work. Its inclusion, therefore, may have the effect of increasing the measured return to hours by allowing this variable to reflect two influences. Hart and Robb (1983) have estimated both production and labour demand functions based on a pooled cross-section/time-series model of the UK manufacturing sector developed from the structure of Model 5.5. Their results indicate strongly both decreasing returns to the labour input and higher returns to workers compared to hours ($\alpha_1 > \alpha_2$).[7]

A somewhat different interpretation of the increasing returns phenomenon is provided by Hart and McGregor (1982). They concentrate on the division of the hours' variable into its standard and overtime components with the former treated as an exogenously determined input and the latter as an endogenous input. One reason for this separation relates to an earlier discussion: thus, standard hours have potentially far higher fixity elements than premium hours. It is further argued that, compared to premium hours, it is less meaningful to treat standard hours as a single factor of production since, in large part, they set the work week for all production factors. Per-period lengths of production runs, business trading hours and machine running times are all strongly influenced by the length of standard work week. This sort of argument leads the authors to test the possibility that standard hours essentially act as a 'scaling' term in the production function. In the event, their results, based on a pooled cross-section/time-series model of FRG manufacturing industry, reveal, for both production and labour demand specifications, significantly lower returns to premium hours compared to workers.[8] Further, their results would seem to indicate important reasons for the need to distinguish between standard and overtime hours in this area of research.

In all, a mere rationalisation of empirical findings of increasing returns to the labour input does not appear to be a satisfactory approach. While the somewhat diverse attempts at model re-specification have yet to be unified, they do point clearly towards the plausibility of the dual assumptions of decreasing returns to the labour input and a higher output elasticity with respect to workers than average hours.

(ii) The Reserve Labour Hypothesis

The models of Oi, Nickell, Okun and others provide cogent reasons to explain why firms may hoard labour during periods around cyclical troughs. Towards cyclical peaks, firms may not employ the number of manhours dictated by short-run product demand considerations. For example, as output grows, uncertainty as to the timing and degree of the next cyclical downturn may well produce increasing caution over undertaking new hiring investments. This quasi-fixity argument is consistent, therefore, with the widely observed empirical phenomenon that manhours vary less than proportionately to output. It may also provide a clue to why high, and even increasing, returns to the labour input are observed. The results may arise from a failure to distinguish between paid-for and effective manhours. High returns may simply reflect the fact that the former measure is generally adopted, and thus the above quasi-fixity effects are picked up, when it would be theoretically more meaningful to attempt some estimate of the latter measure. The best-known example of a researcher measuring and incorporating effective working hours into labour demand functions is Fair (1969). Of course, the reasons why the inclusion of an estimate of capacity utilisation often serves to reduce the estimated returns to labour are closely tied up with the paid-for/effective manhours distinction. In part, capacity utilisation may act as a proxy for the gap between paid-for and effective hours per worker.

Miller (1971) argues strongly that this conceptual problem has been a major reason for confusion over returns to labour input. He attempts to show this indirectly by further developing the reasons for differences between paid-for and effective labour services. In large part, this is carried out within the context of an inventory problem to the firm. The extent to which firms will iron out cyclical fluctuations in product demand by changes in inventories is negatively related to the cost of inventory holdings. The higher such costs, the more likely will be the firm to hold relatively small and stable levels of inventories, while seeking alternative means of dealing with product demand fluctuations. One way may be to hold a 'reserve' of labour, in excess of normal levels, that can be used to meet expected input requirements during peak periods. Obviously, another possibility is to hold excess capital. In its calculation of the relative costs of holding reserves of labour as opposed to inventories and excess capital, the firm will take into account the reduction in hiring/firing and other non-recurring non-wage labour costs. Thus, and strictly in line with Oi's theory, the propensity to hold labour reserves will be expected to be positively related to skill.

The new development here, however, is that, given substitution possibilities between labour and inventories, one would expect labour reserves to be positively correlated with the cost of inventories. This would in turn display itself through a positive correlation between the sizes of industries' output–employment elasticities and their respective inventory costs. Relatively high inventory cost industries will have relatively high labour reserves and, therefore, a larger gap between their recorded (paid-for) manhours and their unrecorded (effective) manhours. This idea is tested for US manufacturing industry, in a two-stage procedure by Miller and, in a somewhat extended analysis, by Greer and Rhoades (1977). In the first stage, they derive output-employment elasticities[9] by industry. The second stage involves undertaking an industry cross-section regression of the elasticity estimates on the cost of inventories, employee skill levels and other relevant variables. The inventory/sales ratio is used as an inverse proxy for inventory costs; *ceteris paribus,* a higher ratio indicates a lower cost of holding inventories. In general, their *a priori* expectations are supported by their subsequent regression estimates.

While the findings seem to highlight a major reason why increasing returns to the labour input are observed, one must nevertheless exercise some caution with these results. The major problems concern the estimation of output–employment elasticities that are derived not from a system, as in (6.6), but rather from simple, single-equation employment functions with either workers or, erroneously in several of the Greer and Rhoades specifications, manhours as the dependent variable. (More recently, a related model developed by Topel, 1982, distinguishes among workers, hours and inventories within the framework of an interrelated factor demand system.) Further, since some of the employment functions include lagged endogenous variables and the estimated elasticities are purged of the short-run adjustment, it is not clear whether or not the output–employment elasticities are short- or long-run estimates. The influence of current inventory costs on long-run output-employment elasticities involves a different set of economic considerations.

6.7 CYCLICAL VARIATIONS IN REGIONAL EMPLOYMENT AND UNEMPLOYMENT

The size of the short-run elasticities of firms' employment and hours responses to a fall in product demand is a function of several variables; from the foregoing discussion we would include the expected length of the demand downturn, the size of non-recurring NWLCs, the skill mix of the workforce and the ratio of productive to non-productive workers. Since, at any point in time, macro economies experience wide geographical variations in these variables, then we might expect spatial cross-sectional variations in the elasticities. Moreover, in relatively 'poor' regions, it might be reasonably conjectured that the values of these variables may be such that, for a given national aggregate demand downturn, relatively high employment–output elasticities and relatively low rates of labour hoarding would be observed. In such regions, one may expect to observe relatively long average spells of unemployment (which, in part, may proxy demand expectations), low proportions of skilled workers, low hiring and training expenditures (owing, in part, to the former two attributes) and small numbers of non-productive workers (owing, for example, to relatively few government and industrial administrative offices).

These and other considerations led Bell and Hart (1980) to derive separate estimates of worker and hours demand functions, similar to those described in section 6.1, for UK regions receiving significant levels of government aid and for the other, more prosperous, regions. This exercise revealed significantly higher employment–output elasticities in the former regions together with significantly lower hours responsiveness to employment disequilibrium. Stated another way, given cyclical demand fluctuations, industries in the poorer regions display a greater recourse to the external labour market and a smaller recourse to the internal labour market than their richer counterparts.

An obvious extension of this approach is to investigate whether such differential regional external/internal labour market responsiveness helps to explain variations in regional unemployment responsiveness to national aggregate demand fluctuations. Such an investigation has been carried out by Bell (1981) for the UK with encouraging results. Other analyses that incorporate regional disparities in non-recurring NWLCs can be found in Cheshire (1981) and Hart (1981).

NOTES

1 There could be other transactions costs of changing hours of work, such as union resistance and organisational/production constraints, but these are discounted here.
2 In this cyclical phase (and its counterpart in the upturn of the cycle), the condition $D > 0$ ($A > 0$) ensures that h is constant, satisfying the constraint that hours times marginal wage costs equals the difference between average wage costs and the discount rate times per-employee dismissal (accession) costs.
3 However, in cycles with long recessionary periods, this picture may well be distorted since the model predicts that, around the trough of the cycle, it is average hours rather than employment that vary with output demand.
4 There are no layoffs in the Salop model in sharp contrast to the Nickell model, which does not allow for quits.
5 Measured as coefficients of variation of employment and hours per worker divided by the coefficient of variation of manhours.
6 Two common restrictions involve using manhours for the labour input (i.e. assuming $\alpha_1 = \alpha_2$) and suppressing c_u ($\alpha_4 = 0$).
7 However, this finding may in part be accounted for by the long-run nature of the time observations in this study, which may have served to 'smooth out' important cyclical features of the data.
8 Two other points are worth noting from this study. First, evidence from micro survey data is quoted that tends generally to refute Feldstein's assertion concerning the relative productivities of overtime and standard hours. Secondly, the authors test most of the different model specifications mentioned in this section and comment on the relative robustness of their various restrictions.

9 Greer and Rhoades actually estimate employment–output elasticities from labour demand functions and find that inverting the elasticities, so as to approximate Miller's original estimates, renders their results insignificant. Explanations are provided for this seeming anomaly.

REFERENCES

Bell, D. N. F. (1981), 'Regional output, employment and unemployment fluctuations', *Oxford Economic Papers,* 33, 42–60.

Bell, D. N. F. (1982), 'Labour utilisation and statutory non-wage costs', *Economica,* 49, 335–343.

Bell, D. N. F. and R. A. Hart (1980), 'The regional demand for labour services', *Scottish Journal of Political Economy,* 27, 140–151.

Berndt, E. R., M. A. Fuss and L. Waverman (1979), 'A dynamic model of costs of adjustment and interrelated factor demand, with an empirical application to energy demand in US manufacturing', *University of British Columbia Discussion Paper,* No. 79–30.

Briscoe, G. and D. A. Peel (1975), 'The specification of the short-run employment function', *Bulletin of the Oxford Institute of Economics and Statistics,* 37, 115–142.

Cheshire, P. C. (1981), 'Labour-market theory and spatial unemployment: the role of demand reconsidered', in R. L. Martin (ed.), *Regional Wage Inflation and Unemployment,* London: Pion Ltd.

Craine, R. (1973), 'On the service flow from labour', *Review of Economic Studies,* 40, 39–46.

Fair, R. C. (1969), *The Short-Run Demand for Workers and Hours,* Amsterdam: North Holland.

Feldstein, M. S. (1967), 'Specification of the labour input in the aggregate production function', *Review of Economic Studies,* 34, 375–386.

Gordon, R. J. (1982), 'Wages and prices are not always sticky: a century of evidence for the US, UK and Japan', *National Bureau of Economic Research,* Cambridge, Mass.: Working Paper No. 847.

Greer, D. F. and S. A. Rhoades (1977), 'A test of the reserve labour hypothesis', *The Economic Journal,* 87, 290–299.

Hart, R. A. (1981), 'Regional wage-change transmission and the structure of regional wages and unemployment', in R. L. Martin (ed.), *Regional Wage Inflation and Unemployment,* London: Pion Ltd.

Hart, R. A. and P. G. McGregor (1982), 'The returns to labour services in West German manufacturing industry', Berlin: International Institute of Management, mimeo.

Hart, R. A. and A. L. Robb (1983), 'Production and labour demand functions with endogenous fixed worker costs', Berlin: International Institute of management, mimeo.

Hart, R. A. and T. Sharot (1978), 'The short-run demand for workers and hours: a recursive model', *Review of Economic Studies,* 45, 299–309.

Kirwan, F. X. (1979), 'Non-wage costs, employment and hours of work in Irish manufacturing industry', *Economic and Social Review,* 10, 231–254.

Leslie, D. and T. Wise (1980), 'The productivity of hours in UK manufacturing and production industries', *The Economic Journal,* 90, 85–94.

McIntosh, J. (1983), 'Dynamic, interrelated factor demand systems: the United Kingdom, 1950–1978', *Conference Papers,* A Supplement to the *Economic Journal,* 78–85.

Miller, R. L. R. (1971), 'The reserve labour hypothesis: some tests of its implications', *The Economic Journal,* 81, 17–35.

Nadiri, M. I. and S. Rosen (1969), 'Interrelated factor demand functions', *American Economic Review,* 59, 457–471.

Nadiri, M. I. and S. Rosen (1974a), *A Disequilibrium Model of Demand for Factors of Production,* New York: National Bureau of Economic Research.

Nadiri, M. I. and S. Rosen (1974b), 'A disequilibrium model of demand for factors of production', *American Economic Review* (Papers and Proceedings), 64, 264–270.

Nickell, S. J. (1978), 'Fixed costs, employment and labour demand over the cycle', *Economica,* 45, 329–345.

Oi, W. (1962), 'Labor as a quasi-fixed factor', *Journal of Political Economy,* 70, 538–555.

Okun, A. M. (1981), *Prices and Quantities,* Oxford: Basil Blackwell.

Pencavel, J. H. (1972), 'Wages, specific training, and labour turnover in US manufacturing industries', *International Economic Review,* 13, 53–64.

Rosen, S. (1968), 'Short-run employment variation on class-I railroads in the US, 1947–1963', *Econometrica,* 36, 511–529.

Salop, S. C. (1973), 'Wage differentials in a dynamic theory of the firm', *Journal of Economic Theory,* 6, 321–344.

Soligo, R. (1966), 'The short-run relationship between employment and output', *Yale Economic Essays,* 6, 161–215.

Tatom, J. A. (1980), 'The "problem" of procyclical real wages and productivity', *Journal of Political Economy,* 88, 385–394.

Topel, R. H. (1982), 'Inventories, layoffs and the short-run demand for labor', *American Economic Review,* 72, 769–787.

7 Wage Inflation and Wage Rigidities

Two aspects of the discussion of the cyclical employment effects of non-wage labour costs would appear to have some considerable bearing on the analysis of wage determination. First, several of the models suggest a cyclical relationship between actual and desired levels of workers and hours and, therefore, may be deemed to be relevant to the cyclical features of wage-change functions that incorporate excess manhour arguments. Second, the trade-off between wages and quit rates and its relationship to Okun's toll suggests the possibility that fixed, non-recurring NWLCs may play some part in the explanations of relative wage responsiveness to cyclical falls in product demand. An examination of these two topics, in sections 7.1 and 7.2 respectively, forms the major content of this chapter.

In a somewhat more direct sense, however, NWLCs would be expected to feature in this general area of research. Wage negotiation, especially in the union sector, features not only direct wages, such as standard, premium and bonus rates of pay, but also fringe benefits and holiday entitlements. Mitchell (1980) provides evidence to support the relative importance of fringes within the total labour compensation package of US unionised firms. Examining coefficients of variation of earnings and fringes (with and without the inclusion of pension schemes) he reveals that, for unionised non-office employees by industry in 1974, the coefficients for fringes are two–three-fold larger than those for earnings. Mitchell goes on to argue that fringe benefit compensation provides unions and employers with the major means of deviating significantly from scheduled earnings patterns established under, particularly longer-term, wage contracts.

Unfortunately, the vast majority of wage determination models exclude any attempt to analyse the role of fringes. Part of the explanation is that detailed fringe benefit data are generally unavailable in most countries. At least two pieces of indirect evidence suggest that this exclusion may be quite critical, however. The first derives from the link, mentioned in Chapter 4 and returned to in Chapter 10, between changes in fringes as a proportion of total worker compensation and the degree of unionisation. Observed econometric differences in the response of wages to price changes, excess demand and other variables given a union/non-union dichotomy of the data may partly reflect the asymmetrical biases of excluding fringes. The second concerns the concept of fringes as protection investments. Where relatively high specific investments are involved, firms may be encouraged to pay fringes (and wage premiums) to discourage quitting (although some limitations are raised to this line of argument in Chapter 10). Now, an observed difference in the performance of wage equations where wages are delineated by length of employment contract may, again, partly reflect the exclusion of fringes. Fringe payments would be expected to feature more importantly alongside longer-term contracts. Evidence of differing wage-change responses to price changes and excess demand given both a union/non-union dichotomy and, especially, a breakdown by contract length is provided by Mitchell (1980). (See also Mitchell and Kimbell, 1982, for more detailed contract evidence.)

Moreover, the sorts of bias that may result from the exclusion of fringes from wage functions would probably not be removed merely by reconstituting the dependent wage variable so as to include fringe payments. A likely role for fringes is that of an endogenous variable within a simultaneous wage determination system. For example, within a union setting, the bargaining model of Freeman (1981) suggests an interaction between wage changes and fringe changes given that fringes have grown in importance within the total compensation package.

In any event, it is of considerable interest to understand the separate effects of exogenous variables on wage and fringe changes. For example, one might wish to test the supply-side argument, suggested by Mabry (1973), that, when vacancies are low relative to unemployment, unions may attempt to protect living standards by bargaining more for fringes than for wages. Rises in the wages variable would attract a relatively high response in labour supply while rises in the fringes variable are 'less visible' to the outside market. It would also be interesting to measure the extent to which firms and workers can circumvent government wage controls by negotiating compensating fringe increases. These sorts of considerations remain largely unexplored and await major new research efforts. More attention has, however, been given to other aspects of the effects of non-wage labour costs on the wage determination process.

7.1 THE CYCLICAL RELATIONSHIP BETWEEN WAGE CHANGES AND UNEMPLOYMENT

The effect of the excess demand for labour services on wage changes continues to be a prime consideration in inflation analysis irrespective of the main theoretical premises that underly each particular model. Moreover, ever since Phillips' original work, it has continued to be popular to refer to recorded unemployment, or perhaps an unemployment/vacancy relationship, as a proxy for excess demand. While this is convenient from theoretical, empirical and policy perspectives, it gives rise to a fundamental problem. Recorded unemployment measures a stock of persons who represent the gap between the number of people who are supplying labour services and those who are actually selling labour services. The problem is that some of those persons who are recorded as employed may also be in the position of supplying more labour services than they are actually selling. For example, at a given wage, employees may be willing to work more hours per week than are actually on offer. A correct definition of unemployment should be in terms of a flow of manhours rather than a stock of persons: it should represent the difference between manhours supplied and manhours actually worked.

Redefining unemployment in this way immediately provides links to the discussion in the previous two chapters. Here, we wish to use several of the earlier developments in order to illustrate the main consequences for the cyclical analysis of wage changes. Two central features emerge. First, the differing cyclical responses of workers and hours to changes in scale variables, induced by the role of fixed NWLCs, have direct implication for the cyclical pattern of wage changes. Second, this cyclical wage behaviour is also conditioned by changes in the relative factor prices of the two components of manhours. The inflation model adopted as background to the present discussion is that of Barro and Grossman (1976) and Grossman (1974). No attempt is made to defend their fixed-price, disequilibrium approach to macro modelling since the main concerns here would be expected to feature in other types of model. The advantage of the Barro and Grossman framework is that it provides the best available example of a system in which excess labour demand is defined in terms of manhours. Barro and Grossman themselves analyse the expected path of wage changes given an exogenous cycle in aggregate excess demand while, in an extension to their model, Hart (1983) considers the implications of changes in relative factor prices. In their derivation of the Phillips curve, Barro and Grossman assume that aggregate (proportional) nominal wage changes, $1/W(\mathrm{d}W/\mathrm{d}t)$, are proportional to aggregate excess demand for labour services ($\bar{L}_x$); thus:

$$\frac{1}{W}\frac{\mathrm{d}W}{\mathrm{d}t} = \lambda(\bar{L}_x) \tag{7.1}$$

where λ is a positive finite speed of adjustment and $\bar{L}_x$ is a weighted average measure of excess demand taken over n markets that are in structural imbalance. As in the models in Chapter 5, it is explicitly recognised that the flow of labour services is a function of both workers and hours per worker. For a single labour market this may be represented by the expression:

$$L_x = g(N^*, h^*) - g(N_{-1}, h_{-1}) \gtreqless 0. \tag{7.2}$$

This measures the difference between the current desired and the previous actual labour services requirement. Note that $L_x = 0$ in (7.2) may occur either because $N^* \equiv N_{-1}$ and $h^* = h_{-1}$ or because N_{-1} and h_{-1} lie on the same isoemployment locus as N^* and h^*.

The relationship between the aggregate unemployment rate and aggregate excess demand is given by:

$$u = u(\overline{L}_x);\ u' < 0, u'' > 0, u^* = u(0) > 0. \tag{7.3}$$

A result, $\overline{L}_x = 0$ implies that the negative excess demand markets in (7.2) exactly counterbalance the positive excess demand markets and, since the unemployment domain has a (theoretical) lower limit of zero, unemployment (u^*) will be positive at $\overline{L}_x = 0$. As $\overline{L}_x$ becomes more positive, and assuming that each market experiences an increase in excess demand, the unemployment rate falls in the markets with negative excess demand for labour services and, at the same time, the number of such markets falls. This produces the inverse, convex relationship implied by the first two restrictions in (7.3). Combining (7.1) and (7.3) gives:

$$u = u\left[\frac{1}{W}\frac{\mathrm{d}W}{\mathrm{d}t}\right]/\lambda \tag{7.4}$$

which, given acceptance of (7.3), maps out the classic Phillips curve; it is negatively sloped and convex with a positive intercept on the u-axis and asymptotic to the $(1/W(\mathrm{d}W/\mathrm{d}t))$-axis.

In order to simulate the cyclical characteristics of the Phillips curve, Barro and Grossman introduce the assumption that, given differences in short-run adjustment costs, a change in the quantity of employment takes the form first of an increase in hours per worker followed by a gradual adjustment of workers. This form of adjustment is a theoretical and/or empirical feature of several of the models discussed in the previous chapter. Here, we combine the 'bare bones' Model 5.1, which excludes capacity utilisation and the capital stock, with the equivalent restricted matrix of factor adjustment taken from (6.6).

This may be written in the form:

$$\begin{aligned} \Delta N &= \beta_{11}(N^* - N_{-1}) + \beta_{12}(h^* - h_{-1}) \\ \Delta h &= \beta_{21}(N^* - N_{-1}) + \beta_{22}(h^* - h_{-1}) \end{aligned} \tag{7.5}$$

where we assume that the hours' average own-adjustment lag, given by $(1 - \beta_{22})/\beta_{22}$, is less than the workers' average own-adjustment lag, $(1 - \beta_{11})/\beta_{11}$. Recall that it is also assumed that equilibrium hours are scale invariant in Model 5.1 (see equation (5.14b)) so that reference can be made to Figure 5.1.

In Figure 5.1 suppose that, given an initial market equilibrium at point A (N_0^*, h_0^* combination of factor inputs), a once-for-all output expansion gives a new desired equilibrium point C (at N_1^*, h_0^*). Excess demand, through (7.2), is positive but is gradually eliminated in the short run along the expansion path A–E rather than the optimum expansion path A–C. Thus, given the assumptions over adjustment constraints in (7.5), hours overshoot their long-run equilibrium level in order to accommodate a shortfall in the actual compared to the equilibrium workforce.

Suppose that the type of differential adjustment response illustrated in Figure 5.1 can be taken to represent the reactions of average aggregate workers and hours per worker in the entire economy. Then, the process becomes particularly interesting at cyclical output turning points. This is illustrated in Figures 7.1(a) and 7.1(b). (See Hansen, 1970, and Grossman, 1974, for alternative derivations incorporating essentially the same concepts.) Consider, as in Figure 7.1(a), that the economy is in the trough of a cycle, with the demand for labour services at $L = L_{\min}$, following a period of continuously falling aggregate output. Given sluggish (downward) employment adjust-

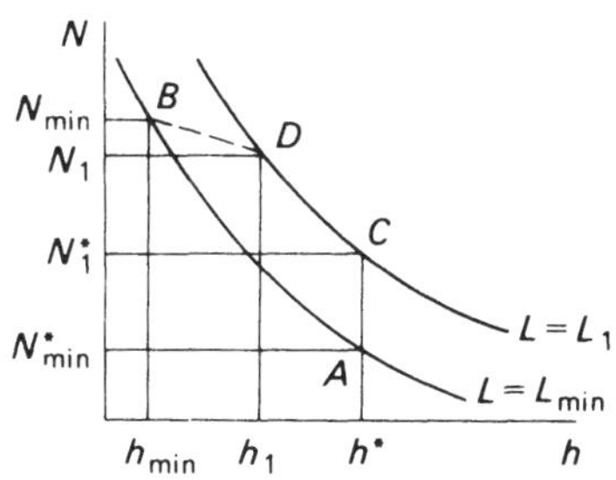

Figure 7.1(a) *Cyclical Trough*

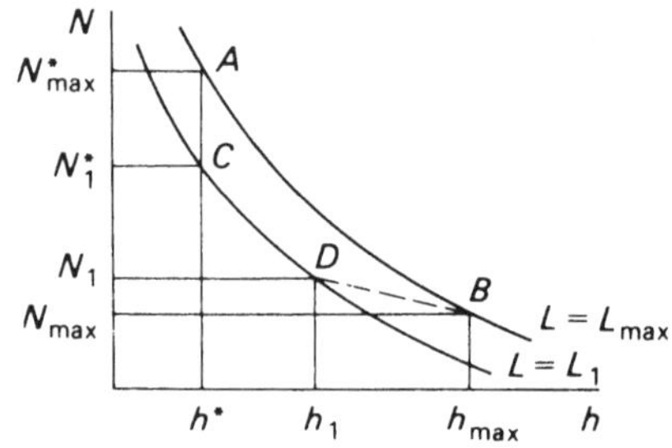

Figure 7.1(b) *Cyclical Peak*

ment, the actual workforce is at point B, which is greater than the desired workforce at point A; that is $N_{min} > N^*_{min}$ with accommodating worker utilisation at $h_{min} < h^*$. Before full adjustment to desired manhours can take place, an upturn in economic activity occurs, which is observed, instantaneously, at $L = L_1$. However, the equilibrium workforce along A–C is always smaller than the actual workforce along B–D since worker adjustment is constrained to move between N_{min} and N_1. In this part of the cycle, therefore, employment continues to fall (unemployment to rise) despite the economic recovery. At the peak of the cycle (see Figure 7.1(b)), on $L = L_{max}$, the actual workforce at point B is less than the desired level at point A. Before full adjustment is achieved, an economic downturn occurs but

Table 7.1 *Counterclockwise loops and the wage-change/unemployment trade-off*

Phase I	*Phase II*
(a) $N^*_t - N_t$ decreasingly negative	(a) $N^*_t - N_t$ increasingly positive
(b) u_t rises since $N^*_t < N_t$	(b) u_t falls since $N^*_t > N_t$
(c) $\frac{1}{W}\frac{dW}{dt}$ rises, through (7.1), as $\bar{L}_x$ rises	(c) $\frac{1}{W}\frac{dW}{dt}$ rises, through (7.1), as $\bar{L}_x$ rises
Phase III	*Phase IV*
(a) $N^*_t - N_t$ decreasingly positive	(a) $N^*_t - N_t$ increasingly negative
(b) u_t falls since $N^*_t > N_t$	(b) u_t rises since $N^*_t < N_t$
(c) $\frac{1}{W}\frac{dW}{dt}$ falls, through (7.1), as $\bar{L}_x$ falls	(c) $\frac{1}{W}\frac{dW}{dt}$ falls through (7.1), as $\bar{L}_x$ falls

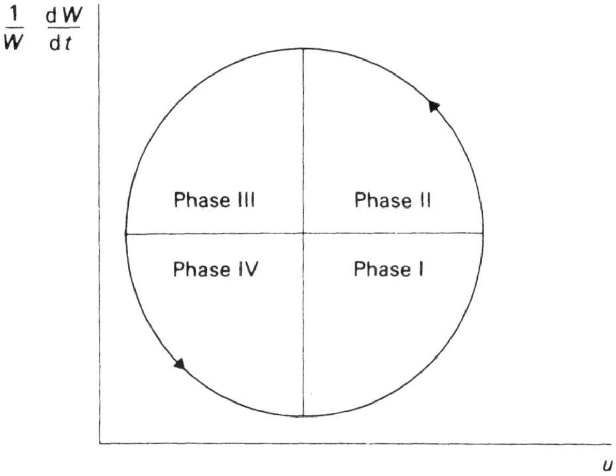

Figure 7.2

in the early stages, such as up to $L = L_1$, the actual workforce adjustment between B and D remains below the desired path A–C. Despite the fall-off in economic activity, employment continues to rise (unemployment to fall).

In terms of the Phillips curve equations, (7.1)–(7.4), this phenomenon provides a systematic displacement of points around the average curve that maps out the classic counterclockwise loops as observed and investigated by Phillips (1958) and many others. This is illustrated succinctly by relating the sketch outlines of four cyclical phases in Table 7.1 to the diagram in Figure 7.2. Clearly Phase II follows completion of the process in Figure 7.1(a), after N^* and h^* have converged and, likewise, Phase IV follows the completion of the process in Figure 7.1(b).

As reported in Chapter 6, Barro and Grossman's assumption of higher adjustment costs in changing the workforce compared to changing average hours is not lacking in theoretical and empirical support. It appears to provide a strong explanation for the oft-observed counterclockwise loops around the Phillips curve. However, except in somewhat special circumstances (see Hart, 1983), the excess demand theories on which the analysis is based seem to stop short of providing insights into why clockwise loops can also be observed, especially in late postwar US data. In line with other writers, Barro and Grossman attempt to explain this particular cyclical phenomenon by means of a price expectations model. Nonetheless, there is a reason for believing that Barro and Grossman underestimate the role of excess demand in helping to explain Phillips curve phenomena. One issue that they do not consider, and that casts considerable doubt on the generality of the restriction in (7.3), is the implication of the fact that, given $\overline{L}_x$ is a function of manhours, excess demand should be analysed not only in terms of changes in output but also with respect to changes in relative factor prices. There are both scale and substitution effects and both can alter the relationship between desired and actual factor inputs. Relative factor prices in our 'bare bones' model are represented by the ratio of fixed/variable labour costs, z_x/v in equations (5.14a) and (5.14b).

Returning to Figure 5.1, at point A (N_0^*, h_0^*), a *ceteris paribus* fall in z_x/v produces, say, a new desired factor combination at B (N_1^*, h_1^*), although in a given short-run period only A–D (< A–B) adjustment is achieved. Note that this pure substitution effect does not produce an excess demand for labour services as defined in (7.2), since we remain on (desired) L_0L_0 with positive excess demand for hours (e.g. $h_1^* - h$) always compensating the negative excess demand for workers (e.g. $N_1^* - N$). However, a much more important consideration is the consequence of contemporaneous changes in both output expectations *and* the ratio of factor prices. Under these circumstances, it is not necessarily the case that the wage inflation–unemployment responses outlined in Table 7.1 will always hold. Here, we illustrate perhaps the most important example of a possible breakdown.

Suppose that the majority of labour markets in a given economy are experiencing sluggish expected output growth as well as relatively large increases in the ratio of fixed to variable labour costs. Indeed, during relatively stagnant economic conditions there often exist special inducements for governments to impose higher fixed NWLC burdens on firms, especially in the areas of financing legislation dealing with job protection and redundancy provisions. In particular, assume that $\overline{L}_x = 0$ with the negative excess demand markets counterbalancing the positive excess demand markets. Through the scale effect, aggregate excess demand for manhours rises but, contemporaneously and following earlier results, there is a desired substitution of more hours per worker for fewer workers. If the substitution effect predominates over the scale effect then positive aggregate excess demand will take the form of an aggregate desire to increase labour utilisation (reduce employment) through a rise in z_x/v more than offsetting the aggregate desire to increase employment due to an increase in Q. This is illustrated in Figure 5.1. Starting at point A (N_0^*, h_0^*), a new equilibrium at point F represents a fall in the workforce due to a rise in z_x/v offsetting the potential shortfall in workers due to a rise in Q. It follows that an increase in the rate of change of nominal wages, a function of the aggregate excess demand for manhours through (7.1) and (7.2) will be associated with an *increase* in the unemployment rate and the relationships in (7.3) and (7.4) break down. An equivalent substitution effect can result from a model that allows more exogenous influences. For example, in Model 5.2 (see equation (5.15)) a fall in standard hours, h_s, has the same effect as a rise in z_x/v. The two effects combined are argued in Hart (1983) to be important contributory factors to the observed breakdown of the Phillips curve in the UK in 1967.

We note at this point that Sheshinski and Weiss (1979) offer an alternative explanation of a positively sloped Phillips curve that involves quasi-fixed NWLCs as a central feature of the model.

It may well be the case in industrial countries that, at least for broad sectors of the economy, z_x/v has displayed trend increases over the past several decades (see Table 2.8) and, certainly, h_s has exhibited a downward trend. For any given rise in z_x/v (fall in h_s), the greater the accompanying rise in Q then the greater the likelihood of observing a predominating scale effect along with the associated Phillips curve phenomena highlighted by Barro and Grossman. The substitution effect may predominate, on the other hand, during stagnating economic conditions with relatively sluggish output growth. In reality, this latter case is probably somewhat 'special' with only few periods in which empirical observations are fully consistent with it. The substitution effect may nonetheless provide some means of distinguishing between relatively strong and relatively weak observed Phillips relationships; in the latter case, the unemployment effects of changes in aggregate output may be considerably dampened by countervailing effects of changes in relative factor prices.

Excess demand defined in terms of manhours and linked to the foregoing labour demand theory seems to provide some insights into the observed cyclical pattern of wages and unemployment as well as into the instability of the Phillips curve. It also strongly suggests that the commonly used excess demand proxies need to be radically improved. Clearly, some distinction has to be made between the demand and supply position for workers on the external market and the demand and supply of hours on the internal market. Further, as we have seen with respect to the reserve labour hypothesis, this distinction should include a separation of effective and paid-for hours. On the internal market, if one merely measures the gap between some calculation of hours supplied and hours paid-for then this may well underestimate the true excess supply of hours since, for reasons established earlier, employers may be hoarding labour.

With these sorts of problem in mind, several authors in their empirical work have attempted to derive proxies for excess demand that capture the above possibilities. Two well-known examples, which adopt a quite distinct methodology for achieving this, are found in Taylor (1970) and Vanderkamp (1972). Taylor's study in particular is quite illuminating. Using US quarterly manufacturing (production worker) data from 1948(4) to 1963(3), he regressed average hourly earnings changes (excluding overtime) on the rate of recorded external unemployment, an estimate of the rate of hidden external unemployment, an estimate of the rate of hoarded internal unemployment as well as other variables familiar to this type of work. The hoarded unemployment variable proves to be very strong, easily outperforming the other two unemployment measures. It actually proves to be a better predictor of wage changes than a composite unemployment measure that encompasses all three influences; Taylor is led to conclude that 'decisions to raise wages are more sensitive to the amount of labour slack within the firm than outside it'. Had Taylor ignored the internal labour market, as most studies continue to do, he would have been forced to argue, at best, that the wage change–unemployment relationship is extremely weak in his sample. In fact, in Taylor's econometrically most sound results, which correct for autocorrelated residuals (see Taylor, 1970, Table III, p. 11), hoarded unemployment is the only significant excess demand measure. It would seem to follow from this type of evidence that writers with a theoretical basis for expecting that the cyclical relationship between nominal wage changes and excess demand will be weak, or non-existent, cannot claim to have tested the alternative hypothesis correctly unless their analysis incorporates the internal labour market. As an interesting footnote to the Taylor study, it is found that external recorded unemployment lags behind the rate of hoarded unemployment by five quarters on the average. This is in line with Barro and Grossman's assumption and with much of Nadiri and Rosen's evidence of labour adjustment generally characterised by speedier changes in hours than in employment.

7.2 WAGE RIGIDITIES

In the Oi/Becker framework (see section 4.1), an unanticipated fall in product demand will produce layoffs that are inversely related to the amount of specific human capital investment per worker. If the demand fall is perceived to be permanent, then the firm will retain those workers whose marginal value product, though reduced, remains above the wage. Higher specific investments produce higher periodic rents. Since, prior to the demand fall, the profit-maximising firm equates marginal value product with the wage plus the periodic rent (see equation (4.4)), then the higher the specificity the less likely is the value of the marginal product to fall below the wage. If, on the other hand, the demand fall is expected to be short-lived, the firm may even be willing temporarily to pay wages that are in excess of marginal value product. It would do this if it estimated that it would earn a positive net return over the life of the investment after subtracting the present value of the loss incurred during the fall-off in demand. In both situations, *ceteris paribus*, workers with specific human capital will not quit their jobs since their wage remains higher than the best alternative wage by the amount of their share of the return to the investment. For a given demand fall, suppose that the firm calculates that it will make a net loss if it retains a given worker. Is there an alternative strategy that might prevent layoff while at the same time benefiting both parties? Without further amendment, the answer from the Oi/Becker model is 'no', since employment provides the only form of adjustment. However, is it not possible for both parties to agree to a wage reduction as an alternative strategy? An answer to this latter question, given the constraint imposed by the former, is suggested by Hashimoto (1975).

Hashimoto develops a two-period model in which he examines the possible employment and wage reactions of a worker and firm given an unanticipated recession. The worker has specific training and the analysis concentrates on the period between the completion of the initial investment and retirement. During this time the worker's 'normal' constant marginal product is reduced by a given constant amount during one recessionary sub-interval. On the assumption of significantly lower costs of acquiring information about product prices than about alternative wages, both parties act as if alternative wages remain unchanged through both periods. Consider the position immediately preceding the recession. (In what follows, wages and marginal products are in terms of present values after discounting to retirement.) The worker receives a wage that represents the best alternative, or opportunity, wage plus a share of the difference between his/her marginal product and the opportunity wage. The increment to the opportunity wage represents the worker's net gain from the specific investment. The firm's net gain from retaining the worker is represented by the difference between the worker's marginal product and the wage. Their combined net gain is the increment to marginal product due to the human capital investment. There now occurs an unanticipated fall in product demand that is then restored after a given interval. In the absence of further assumptions, the worker's net gain remains unchanged. The firm's previous estimation of gain, however, has to be modified since, during the demand fall, the worker's marginal product is reduced. In its revised calculation the firm will have to subtract the capital loss represented by the fall in marginal product. The deeper and/or the longer the recessionary interval, the greater is this loss. Further, the new estimates of net gain both to the firm alone and in combination with the worker can be positive or negative.

Three possibilities now arise. First, the recession is severe enough to render the combined net gain negative. In this case the firm and the worker will separate, either through layoff or quit. Layoffs result from the firm's negative net gain given a zero wage reduction; quits result from the worker's negative net gain given a compensating wage reduction. Second, the employer incurs a negative net gain due to the recession, but the combined gain remains positive. Now, it is both feasible and desirable for the parties to agree to a wage reduction that renders the employer's net gain positive and that reduces the worker's net gain. Third, if the net gain to the firm remains positive the wage is likely to remain fixed. An attempt to regain some of the lost marginal product by a cut in wages is likely to produce additional costs associated with worker hostility as well as loss of credibility and goodwill.

This theory predicts, therefore, that the likelihood of wage reduction increases, and the likelihood of a job separation decreases, the higher the worker's skill specificity. Moreover, given a wage reduction does occur, its size will be positively related both to the level of the worker's specificity and the degree to which the worker shares in the returns to specific investment. Some statistical support for these predictions is obtained by Hashimoto using data on job separations and wage reductions in the Seattle area of the USA during 1971–2.

While this extension at least points towards the lack of generality in the fixed-wage model, it begs a number of important questions. The outcomes hinge on the parties' appraisal of the value of the worker both to the firm and in alternative employment. General human capital can be assumed to enhance the worker's marginal product as much elsewhere as in the firm. The key variable is the value of the worker's marginal product due to specific human capital investment and acquired on-the-job knowledge. Treatment of the problem as if, in any given future time interval, this incremental value is a constant that is accurately measured and agreed upon by both parties is somewhat less than adequate. As suggested in section 4.1, the information costs involved in assessing the value, both to the firm and to its competitors in the labour market, are likely to be considerable. They involve estimates of changes in technological innovation, market conditions, aptitude in acquiring on-the-job skills and so on. Forecast errors will be made and the likelihood of this will influence the parties' approach to formulating wage agreements. The position is aggravated in two further directions. First, the information costs are asymmetrical and mutual agreements on estimates may be difficult to reach. Second, as discussed in some detail by Okun (1981, pp. 83–7), there are potential incentives to each party to misinform the other as to its own true estimates in an attempt to increase its share of the quasi-rent to specific capital. Workers may make quit-threats in order to increase the firm's assessment of the worker's value of marginal product in alternative employment. For its part, the firm may try to underplay its assessment of the worker's marginal product.

One approach towards reducing this last sort of problem may be for the parties to reach a quasi-long-term contractual agreement that pre-specifies the wage over some given future period while allowing unilaterally initiated separation at any time. However, this increases the chances of the type of resource loss discussed in Hashimoto (1975). Layoffs and quits may occur despite the possibility of joint positive shares of the quasi-rent. A long-term contract, pre-specifying the wage while allowing neither side to initiate separation, would overcome this type of resource loss. However, it might increase the adjustment costs involved in optimally reallocating the worker, under a new contractual arrangement, in the event of a discrepancy between expected and actual productivity outcomes. Between these possibilities, no layoff (or tenure) contracts and no-quit (or indenture) contracts produce potentially serious problems of moral hazard (Okun, 1981, pp 87–8).

An investigation of optimum wage strategies given the problems of both the information costs of determining the size of the quasi-rent to specific human capital and the costs of specifying a contract that allocates the division of the quasi-rent is undertaken by Hashimoto (1979, 1981) and Hashimoto and Yu (1980). A two-period model dichotomises between investment and post-investment periods. Initially the worker is endowed with general human capital (k_g), which is assumed to remain fixed in value. The cost of acquiring firm-specific human capital (k_s) on the job is given by:

$$C = C(k_s) \; C' > 0, C'' > 0. \tag{7.6}$$

The firm values its product per unit of k_s as $(m + \eta)$ where m is a constant and η is a density function $\theta(\eta)$ with $E(\eta) = 0$. The value per unit of k_s in alternative employment is also described by a random variable, ϵ, with density function $\psi(\epsilon)$ and $E(\epsilon) = 0$. Thus, η and ϵ represent the prediction errors mentioned above and, for simplicity, it is assumed that $\mathrm{Cov}(\eta, \epsilon) = 0$. In the post-investment period, the value of the worker's marginal product is given to the firm by:

$$v = k_g + (m + \eta)k_s \tag{7.7}$$

and in its alternative employment by:

$$y = k_g + (\epsilon)k_s. \tag{7.8}$$

The firm's quasi-rent is thus:

$$R = v - y = (m + \eta - \epsilon)k_s. \tag{7.9}$$

The worker's wage is given by:

$$\omega = y + \alpha(v - y) \; 0 \leq \alpha \leq 1 \tag{7.10}$$

where α is the share of the returns to specific human capital. A fixed wage, $\bar{\omega}$, would be set at:

$$\bar{\omega} = k_g + \alpha m k_s \tag{7.11}$$

which incorporates the expected values of the random variables. At the other extreme, a completely flexible (or spot-contract) wage is represented by:

$$\omega = k_g + \epsilon k_s + \alpha(m + \eta - \epsilon)k_s. \tag{7.12}$$

The operation of the wage formula in (7.12) would require the parties to reach full and costless agreement on the actual values of η and ϵ. Suppose initially that no such agreement is forthcoming and that a decision is made to operate with the fixed-wage formula in (7.11) over some interval of time. The length of interval may be chosen with regard to minimising the costs associated with frequent competitive wage bargaining while allowing for periodic settlements that enable the parties to 'catch up' with realised productivity changes. Now, under the operation of this fixed-wage contract, the parties would mutually agree to separate if $R < 0$ in (7.9), or:

$$m \leq \epsilon - \eta. \tag{7.13}$$

Workers would quit if $\bar{\omega} - y \leq 0$ or, substituting from (7.8) and (7.10),

$$\alpha m \leq \epsilon. \tag{7.14}$$

The firm would dismiss workers if $v - \bar{\omega} \leq 0$ or, substituting from (7.7) and (7.11),

$$(1 - \alpha)m \leq -\eta. \tag{7.15}$$

The separation rules in (7.13), (7.14) and (7.15) reveal that optimal separation under this fixed-wage contract occurs only on the average; that is, at the expected values of η and ϵ. Resource losses occur when workers are laid off or quit despite a positive quasi-rent. Given the constraint of the fixed wage, it is in the best interests of the parties to agree on a sharing ratio, α, that minimises these losses.

An alternative strategy is to attempt to reach contractual agreements that allow more flexibility in the wage. Essentially this requires the parties to obtain estimates $\hat{\eta}$ and $\hat{\epsilon}$ in (7.12) based on mutually acceptable indicators of post-investment productivities. The poorer are these indicators or the lower the agreement over their appropriateness, the more the wage in (7.12) approaches its fixed-wage special case in (7.11). Hashimoto and Yu (1980) confirm the intuitively plausible result that a partially pre-specified flexible wage based on indicators that reflect some of the expected productivity change reduces the resource loss associated with the fixed wage. Indirect evidence that the parties do indeed adopt partial flexibility, at least with respect to estimates of η, is perhaps to be found in those instances where special bonus schemes are adopted that periodically adjust wages to reflect agreed-upon productivity gains. Perhaps the best-known example of this approach is the Japanese bonus payment system, which relates, primarily, to Japanese workers with long tenure. Hashimoto (1979) has tested the possibility that Japanese wages bonuses are positively associated with changes in productivity arising from specific human capital investment with some affirmative results.

As indicated earlier, alongside changes in α and the use of economic indicators, resource losses are also affected by the type of contract selected and, in particular, by how each type of contract influences layoff and quit rules. In a simulation exercise, Hashimoto and Yu (1980) compare optimum properties of long-term, quasi-long-term, tenure and indenture contracts given changes in the quality of the economic indicators used to assess η and ϵ. Optimisation involves finding values of α and k_s that maximise joint net wealth. While some interesting differences in these values occur among the four types of contract, the authors' general conclusion about the relationship between wage flexibility and specific investments is of most relevance to the present discussion. Within a given firm, the tendency is for higher specific human capital to be associated with more wage flexibility. In (7.12), with m given, a higher k_s increases the marginal gain, which, in turn, increases the incentive to the parties to improve the economic indicators used to estimate η and ϵ. They will adopt this strategy so long as the marginal costs of improvement do not fully offset the marginal gains of increased k_s. Across industries, m cannot be taken as given and, in general, the greater the value of m the lower the wage flexibility. This occurs because a larger m decreases the relative importance of η and ϵ and thus decreases the marginal gains to improved indicators.

There would seem to be much potential in this human capital approach to wage flexibility. However, a number of issues, outside the Hashimoto and Yu framework, will need to be accommodated in future work before unequivocal relationships can be established. One relates to the possibility suggested by Okun (see section 6.4) that the problems associated with the firm's wage strategy may concern the likelihoods of non-optimal separations not only during the slump period but in a future tight market position. Workers may quit in better times if they feel that the firm reneged on past (implicit) commitments to maintain wages. Another, more important, issue relates to the comparison of the relative advantages of price- and quantity-adjustment modes. The latter involves changes in quits and layoffs *but also* changes in hours of work per worker. Given specific investments, the degree to which average hours are adjusted downward, *à la* Nickell-type model, rather than wages would seem to be a consideration of some critical importance. Finally, the relative attraction of the quantity-adjustment mode will be improved if the probability of recall is increased and thus the loss of specific investments reduced. Such a possibility would seem to be provided by an employment insurance system that is less than perfectly experience-rated. However, this may not damage the association between specific investments and wage flexibility if layoff follows inverse seniority rules. Since workers with relatively high specific human capital are likely to be encouraged to have the longest job tenure, then they may be largely unaffected by temporary layoffs, owing to unemployment insurance. In any case, for reasons discussed in the next chapter, the phenomenon of temporary layoff as a means of combating short-run recessionary periods is not of particularly significant quantitative importance throughout OECD countries.

Finally, we note a recent addition to the literature on wage rigidity (Plessner and Yitzhaki, 1983) that utilises a somewhat wider definition of quasi-fixed labour costs. Their approach involves a profit-maximising firm that distinguishes between workers and hours per worker in an equivalent fashion to that incorporated, for example, in Model 5.1. An important aspect of their framework involves distinguishing between two types of quasi-fixed cost. The first comprises the once-over costs involved in hiring and training workers. The second, referred to as 'employee carrying costs', covers those recurring costs associated with the administration of the payroll, canteen and recreation facilities and certain types of fringe benefit. Unlike once-over costs, carrying costs are contingent on workers remaining in employment. Defining an hourly wage cost that would normally be expected to vary positively with the length of the work-day, the authors derive conditions for the relative responsiveness of workers and hours per worker (and, thus, hourly wages) for changes in product price. Their results are divided into two parts depending on whether their per-worker cost function is defined in terms of once-over *or* recurring fixed costs. Conditions are derived for which it is optimal for the firm to respond to a fall in product price by reducing employment rather than hours and wages. The key results would appear to hinge on the size of the rate of change of marginal hiring and carrying costs for which, unfortunately, it is hard to obtain hard information. However, as indicated by the type of studies mentioned in section 6.5, there is considerable macro evidence that average hours do vary quite sharply in the short run and this perhaps casts doubt on the overall importance of the results. On the other hand, the study is interesting in that it strongly suggests that, by broadening the definition of quasi-fixed costs to include recurring elements, the generality of Hashimoto's approach (which concentrates, essentially, on once-over costs) may be brought into question.

REFERENCES

Barro, R. J. and H. I. Grossman (1976), *Money, Employment and Inflation*, Cambridge: Cambridge University Press.

Freeman, R. B. (1981), 'The effect of unionism on fringe benefits', *Industrial and Labor Relations Review*, 34, 489–509.

Grossman, H. I. (1974), 'The cyclical pattern of unemployment and wage inflation', *Economica*, 41, 403–413.

Hansen, B. (1970), 'Excess demand, unemployment, vacancies, and wages', *The Quarterly Journal of Economics*, 84, 1–23.

Hart, R. A. (1983), 'The Phillips curve and cyclical manhour variation', *Oxford Economic Papers*, 35, 186–201.

Hashimoto, M. (1975), 'Wage reduction', unemployment and specific human capital', *Economic Inquiry*, 13, 485–504.

Hashimoto, M. (1979), 'Bonus payments, on-the-job training, and lifetime employment in Japan', *Journal of Political Economy*, 87, 1086–1104.

Hashimoto, M. (1981), 'Firm-specific human capital as a shared investment', *American Economic Review*, 71, 475–482.

Hashimoto, M. and B. T. Yu (1980), 'Specific capital, employment contracts, and wage rigidity', *The Bell Journal of Economics*, 11, 536–549.

Mabry, B. (1973), 'The economics of fringe benefits', *Industrial Relations*, 12, 95–106.

Mitchell, D. J. B. (1980), *Wages, Unions and Inflation*, Washington, DC: The Brookings Institution.

Mitchell, D. J. B. and L. J. Kimbell (1982), 'Labor market contracts and inflation', in M. N. Baily (ed.), *Workers, Jobs, and Inflation*, Washington DC: The Brookings Institution.

Okun, A. M. (1981), *Prices and Quantities*, Oxford: Basil Blackwell.

Phillips, A. W. (1958), 'The relationship between unemployment and the rate of change of money wage rates in the United Kingdom, 1861–1957', *Economica*, 25, 283–299.

Plessner, Y. and S. Yitzhaki (1983), 'Unemployment and wage rigidity: the demand side', *Oxford Economic Papers*, 35, 202–212.

Sheshinski, E. and Y. Weiss (1979), 'Demand for fixed factors, inflation and adjustment costs', *The Review of Economic Studies*, 46, 31–45.

Taylor, J. (1970), 'Hidden unemployment, hoarded labor, and the Phillips curve', *The Southern Economic Journal*, 37, 1–16.

Vanderkmap, J. (1972), 'Wage adjustment, productivity and price change expectations', *The Review of Economic Studies*, 39, 61–72.

8 Unemployment Insurance, Other Obligatory Social Welfare Contributions and Unemployment

The bulk of the firm's obligatory social welfare contributions are comprised of three broad items, which are, ranked in descending order of importance (see Table A2.8), old age benefit, sickness benefit and unemployment insurance. Changes in per-worker contributions take the form of changes in payroll tax rates and/or changes in the contribution ceilings. Despite the quantitative importance of these items within the firm's total labour bill, a relatively small part of the social welfare literature has been devoted to analysing their effects on the firm's employment behaviour. Rather, it has concentrated on the benefit or supply side of the labour market, examining the effects of changes in benefits on such variables as intensity of search activity, labour force participation, temporary layoffs and work effort. The effects of contribution changes are of interest not only because they too have employment implications but also because benefit and contribution changes often occur contemporaneously, especially in schemes with self-financing objectives. The question of particular interest that then arises is whether the employment effects of contribution changes complement or counteract those of benefit changes. In illustrating some of the complications involved in incorporating the contribution side, we first concentrate on unemployment insurance in section 8.1. Emphasis is given to differences between the US contribution system and those generally observed elsewhere. The discussion is then widened in Section 8.2 to include other obligatory contributions. Section 8.3 assesses the implications of allowing for the employment effects of changes in social welfare contributions for related supply-side studies into the determinants of the rate of unemployment. Finally, some brief general conclusions are given in section 8.4.

8.1 LAYOFFS AND UNEMPLOYMENT INSURANCE CONTRIBUTIONS

Perhaps the two best-known papers that have developed relationships between unemployment insurance (UI) benefits and layoffs are those of Feldstein (1976) and Baily (1977) (F–B for short). Among the many related contributions are those of Feldstein (1973; 1975; 1978) and Topel and Welch (1980). In the traditional job search theory, an unemployed worker endeavours to find a wage that is greater than the optimal reservation wage after voluntarily quitting the previous job or being involuntarily laid off. The F–B theory, however, plays down the importance of involuntary layoff followed by job search. Feldstein, in particular, claims that the typical US worker appears to be laid off for a relatively short period before returning to his/her former employer; thus, he summarises the recent position:

> In manufacturing, about 75 per cent of those who are laid off return to their original employers. More generally, among all workers classified as 'unemployed job losers', temporary layoffs account for about 50 per cent of all unemployment spells. Temporary layoffs are an even larger fraction of cyclical changes in the number of job losers (Feldstein, 1978 p. 834).

In the F–B theory, the firm chooses an efficient labour contract or contingent rules for adjusting employment. They consider the profit-maximising firm's demand for labour when workers who are hired have a positive probability of being laid off during some future time interval. This probability together with wages, unemployment benefit, hours of work and expected layoff duration enters the worker's utility function. The firm's optimising behaviour, given competitive conditions, is constrained to keep the worker's total utility constant. Suppose that the unemployment benefit system is less than fully experience-rated. With a rise in UI benefit, *ceteris paribus*, both workers and the firm will realise a gain. Workers' utility rises since total expected compensation is increased. Moreover, the firm's contribution to this increase is effectively subsidised since some part of the cost is borne by other firms through a general levy and/or through general government revenues. In order to realise this gain, while at the same time maintaining the constant-utility rule, firms will increase layoffs.

Overlooking the effects of changes in taxes on wage income and benefit income, two central predictions arise from the F–B theory. Layoffs will increase with a *ceteris paribus* rise in unemployment benefit or with a *ceteris paribus* fall in the degree of experience rating. The first prediction is tested by Feldstein (1978), while tests of the second can be found in Brechling (1981).

Feldstein further argues that the inducement to temporary layoff provided by UI schemes is likely to be enhanced if the firm's workforce is unionised. The facts that unions can often achieve compensation above market rates, seniority privileges, and special, though firm-related, pension rights will serve to increase the expectation to the employer of return after layoff. Also, union members themselves are usually more confident of recall after layoff, and so less averse to being laid off, since they can often negotiate contracts that stipulate that they will be re-employed by the firm before other job offers are made.

Empirical support for these contentions is presented by Medoff (1979) in a study of the effects of unionisation on UI and layoffs in both two-digit and three-digit US industries. Medoff's results strongly indicate that unionised firms, when trying to achieve labour reductions, exhibit a much higher propensity to use layoffs rather than to rely on quits, real wage cuts, average hours reductions and discharges. On the other hand, labour adjustment in non-unionised firms seems to be achieved more through quit–rehire than through layoff–recall, although the latter combination plays some role.

The emphasis on the importance of short spells of unemployment has been vigorously challenged in recent times with respect to the US experience (Clark and Summers, 1979; Akerlof and Main, 1981) as well as to that of the UK (Main, 1982) and FRG (Freiburghaus, 1978). The thrust of the attack concerns the measurement and interpretation of an unemployment spell-length and it has been convincingly shown that short spells of, say, three months or less make up a fairly negligible proportion of the aggregate unemployment rate.

Another source of evidence casts doubt on the Feldstein–Baily–Medoff arguments. In Europe and Japan, as compared with the USA, there is relatively little resort to temporary layoffs (see Moy and Sorrentino, 1981) and yet, given the F–B predictions, it might have been expected that proportionately *more* European temporary layoffs would have been observed. Compared to the USA there is less experience rating (usually, in fact, no experience rating at all), a higher proportion of the workforce is eligible for benefits, which are generally higher, and trade unions are both better developed and represent a far higher proportion of the workforce. FitzRoy and Hart (1983) have examined a number of factors that may explain this difference between the USA and elsewhere, one of which involves UI contributions as an obligatory non-wage labour cost to the firm. While their analysis is also conducted within an efficient-contract framework, the main arguments can be conveniently represented by reference to two of the 'myopic' models outlined in Chapter 5, thereby following the approach adopted in Hart (1982). Reference will then be made to the equivalent efficient-contract results.

Under almost every scheme in OECD countries, firms experience UI as a statutory imposed tax on their taxable payroll. Ignoring the problem of experience rating, the basic payment method is the same. The firm contributes to UI in the form of a tax on a worker's earnings up to a ceiling limit. For workers with earnings below a given ceiling, the tax constitutes a variable, earnings-related employment cost. For workers with earnings above the ceiling, the tax takes the form of a fixed employment cost. Changes in the per capita contribution rate can occur, through changes in the payroll tax rate and/or changes in the ceiling limit.

In practice, however, the *application* of the US system compared with most of the others elsewhere differs in one fundamental respect. Currently, under federal and forty state programmes, the ceiling limit is set at $6,000 a year, which is less than half average earnings. In almost all other countries, on the other hand, the ceiling is considerably higher than the average. Table 2.5 illustrates the position as far as the four countries of interest here are concerned by showing (see column 3) the ratio of UI ceilings to average earnings; a ratio of under 0.5 in the USA contrasts with ratios in excess of 1.5 in the other countries. That the latter ratios represent, for the typical worker, variable labour costs is amply illustrated for the UK and FRG in Tables 2.6 and 2.7 and the associated discussion. By contrast, the US ratio appears to indicate that UI contributions are a fixed worker cost. As mentioned in Chapters 2 and 5, however, there is a further complicating factor in the US payroll tax system. Since the UI tax is non-transferable, the greater the turnover rate in a given job then the higher is the effective tax ceiling.

What are the employment implications of increases in firms' payroll tax rates and/or ceiling limits assuming that a significant proportion of the increase, at least in the short run, is not passed on in the form of lower wages? (See the discussion in section 4.5.) The core of Brechling's (1977) employment analysis of the US system is represented in Model 5.3. The cost function (equation 5.16) is a variant of the simpler case in Model 5.1, designed to accommodate the turnover complication. Indeed, the extreme positions of no quits ($q' = 0$) in (5.17) and no ceiling ($\widetilde{\omega} = v'h$) in (5.18) reduce the cost function to the equivalent of that in Model 5.1 since they imply that the contributions comprise purely fixed and variable worker costs, respectively. There is little doubt that the appropriate US model 'tends to' expression (5.17), given the strong evidence (see Hall, 1982) that a large majority of workers remain in their jobs for two years or more. As for the European/Japanese position, expression (5.18) is a near-approximation to the typical firm, given the relative high ceilings.

In order to appreciate the overall employment consequences of changes in UI, it is useful to consider contemporaneous changes in benefits and contributions. Generally, secular growth in UI rates of benefit has been accompanied by growing UI contribution rates and ceilings. At least two factors account for this. First, many countries have designed schemes with the aim of achieving full or significant partial self-financing. Second, in most European countries, a specific design feature of the UI systems ensures an automatic positive relationship between benefit and contribution growth rates. This occurs because, given eligibility, benefits are related to previous earnings for a period of time after the commencement of a spell of unemployment. As has been previously established, contributions are also largely related to earnings in these countries.

How do we assess the demand and supply reactions to changes in UI given the assumption that benefit and contribution changes are positively correlated? On the demand side, the key variable is the ratio of fixed to variable worker costs, z_x/v, given that equations (5.17) and (5.18) allow us, in effect, to adopt Model 5.1. This, of course, overlooks the complications introduced by more elaborate model specifications. On the supply side, the corresponding key variable, which is common to much of the research work, is the benefit replacement ratio, b/y, where b is the unemployment benefit and y is the net income received from employment. We note that the 'correct' construction of b/y is a matter of some considerable debate (for example, see Burdett, 1979, and Nickell, 1979, for two possibilities) and, indeed, that there is a theoretical questionmark over its appropriateness (Harrison and Hart, 1983b). Notwithstanding, it is used here for convenience of exposition and without damaging the central arguments. Following F–B, an increase in b/y, *ceteris paribus*, would be expected to reduce employment and increase (temporary) layoffs. It might also be noted that Feldstein (1976) examines theoretically the effects of b/y on layoffs when both workers and hours can be varied in the firm; a rise in b/y decreases employment and increases average hours worked per worker. An important aspect of the *joint* influence of the two ratios is whether the UI contributions constitute a fixed, variable or mixed fixed/variable worker cost to the firm. Three possibilities are considered in turn, omitting, for the present, changes in the wage ceiling.

(i) Per-Worker Unemployment Insurance Contributions

Here the firm's per-period contributions depend only on the size of the workforce and are independent of changes in the individual payroll. This might occur because of the imposition of a crude lump-sum per capita tax or because the wage ceiling is so low that all workers' earnings are above the ceiling. The first example epitomises the early interwar UK schemes, while the latter provides a fair approximation to a US firm with a relatively low turnover rate.

Contributions in this form comprise a part of *fixed* NWLCs. Thus, a contemporaneous increase in benefits and contributions will lead, *ceteris paribus*, to an increase in both b/y and z_x/v. The rise in z_x/v will induce the firm to reduce its desired workforce. This result, therefore, will tend to *reinforce* the employment effects of the rise in b/y. Any tendency, *à la* F–B, to increase temporary layoffs will be magnified by the desire to substitute more hours for fewer workers. Of course, in the absence of other assumptions, it is not possible to comment on the degree to which the labour adjustment under the relative factor price change will take the form of layoffs or natural wastage. Brechling (1977), for example, shows that, under the reserve ratio method of experience rating, an increase in the UI tax encourages the use of voluntary quits when downward employment adjustment is warranted.

(ii) Per-Manhour Unemployment Insurance Contributions

This position corresponds to most European countries and Japan, where the UI payroll tax represents mainly a variable labour cost. In this case, a contemporaneous increase in benefits and contributions will lead to an increase in b/y but a reduction in z_x/v. The higher propensity to resort to temporary layoffs due to the higher benefit would be *offset* by an increase in the desired workforce compensated for by a reduction in average hours of work. The net employment effect is indeterminate, depending on relative parameter sizes.

(iii) Mixed Per-Worker/Per-Manhour Unemployment Insurance Contributions

US firms with relatively high turnover rates and European/Japanese firms with relatively high earnings would be expected to face UI contributions that are partly fixed and partly variable. The essential point is that, under a 'mixed' scheme, a contemporaneous increase in benefits and contributions will induce temporary layoffs through the F–B effect but may increase or decrease desired employment due to the factor price effect; this depends on whether the per-worker or the per-manhour part of the tax prevails. Brechling (1977, pp 70–6) gives a formal comparative static analysis of the factor price effects in this situation.

We would expect changes in wage ceilings, as opposed to contribution rates, to have a much more significant impact in the USA than in European countries. Given such relatively low ceiling ratios in the USA, any conceivable rise in the ceiling level[1] would produce an unambiguous increase in z_x/v. Per-worker fixed labour costs would rise by the ceiling increase multiplied by the UI payroll tax rate. This occurs because, with the exception of a few marginal cases, each worker's annual earnings would remain above the new ceiling level. In Europe, on the other hand, the outcome of the ceiling increase is both more complicated and less conclusive. As we have already noted, relatively few workers' earnings are above the European ceilings. A proportion of these would remain above the new ceiling level with, as in the typical US case, associated fixed-cost increases producing a rise in z_x/v. Others, on the other hand, who *were* above the old ceiling will *now* be below the new ceiling. Their UI labour costs will switch from fixed to variable, thus producing an offsetting fall in z_x/v. Since the earnings distribution above any given ceiling will be markedly positively skewed, the overall effect of a ceiling change is likely to be negligible.

As in Medoff's temporary layoff analysis, the union/non-union dichotomy may have some important bearing on the z_x/v effect, particularly in Europe. Since, on the average, unionised workers enjoy earnings that are above market-determined levels, a significantly larger proportion of such workers may be *above* a given ceiling level than their non-unionised counterparts. In this event, the implications in section 8.1(i) above may have relevance to some of the strongly unionised European sectors. As for US unions, we note from Freeman (1981) that unionised workers are better able to increase the fringe benefit share of total compensation than are non-unionised workers. Since fringes have a high fixity element, this tendency may serve to enhance the effects in section 8.1(i) for unionised workers (see Chapter 10, below). Also, evidence from the USA (Freeman, 1980; Medoff, 1979) that union members have a lower propensity to quit their jobs even when wages and fringes are held constant increases the likelihood, given the structure of Model 5.3, of a high fixity element within changes in UI contributions in unionised firms.

FitzRoy and Hart (1983) have examined UI financing within an efficient-contract model. The assumption is made that the firm maximises profits while holding the expected utility of workers constant in order to capture the idea that rational workers consider not only the going wage rate but also the prospective stability of employment. The further constraint is imposed that, on average, UI is self-financing. The foregoing results are modified somewhat within the new model structure but the essential difference between the USA and elsewhere remains unchanged. Thus, within this model structure, while more layoff unemployment is generated for a rise in benefits financed *either* by a per-head tax *or* by a variable payroll tax, the latter tax has *less* quantitative impact than the former.

Of the main three social welfare contributions, UI costs are the lowest faced by the firm; typically, they account for 1–2 per cent of total labour costs. Therefore, while the foregoing arguments are consistent with the relative difference in temporary layoff experience in the USA and elsewhere, probably they provide no more than a partial explanation. They do point to the fact, however, that those econometric studies that have attempted to measure the effect of b/y on layoffs may suffer from mis-specification biases if contribution effects are ignored. This may be particularly serious if self-financing occurs, with strong (positive or negative) correlations between b/y and z_x/v. A more specific example of such mis-specification is given in section 8.3. First, however, we deal with the obvious, but important, point that if all social welfare costs are considered, then the quantitative impact of the contribution effects on layoffs and hours of work may be increased considerably.

8.2 OTHER OBLIGATORY SOCIAL WELFARE CONTRIBUTIONS

It is often the case that the UI contribution rates and ceilings are not changed in isolation but occur within a 'package' of broader obligatory social welfare tax-rate and ceiling changes. An obvious case in point is the UK, where one tax rate and ceiling limit applies to all such payments. As is evident from Table 2.5, the ceiling levels on European and Japanese old age pension and sickness benefits are also high in relation to average earnings and so, in general, the effects of tax-rate and ceiling changes would be in line with those discussed in relation to UI contributions. Again, tax-rate changes provide clearer outcomes than ceiling changes. Bell (1982) has investigated theoretically the effects on labour utilisation of changes in statutory NWLCs for all combinations of earnings, ceilings and hours levels. His analysis allows for ceiling earnings to be above or below earnings during standard hours and then for all the possible levels of actual hours worked in relation both to standard and to ceiling-equivalent hours of work. He acknowledges that the typical combination in OECD countries is for average hours to be in excess of standard hours and for average wages to be less than social welfare wage ceilings. This leads him to conclude:

> For those [employees] above the ceiling an increase in the contribu-

> tion rate will increase fixed costs vis-à-vis variable costs, while for those below the ceiling the reverse will be the case. Given that the great majority of employees will be below the ceiling wage the net effect of such an increase will promote employment at the expense of utilisation. (Bell, 1982, p. 342)

In line with the discussion above, Bell finds that the effects of increases in the ceiling levels are somewhat more ambiguous.

If unemployment benefit increases are accompanied not only by increased UI contribution tax rates and ceilings but also by increases in other social security contributions, then the potency of the 'contribution effect' in section 8.1 in offsetting the 'benefit effect' may be considerably enhanced.

We note that in the US social welfare system the OASDHI contributions are also epitomised by high ceiling levels (see Table 2.5). In this case, the increased layoff effect for an increase in UI benefits and contributions would be offset by a worker-for-hours substitution effect given a general rise in social welfare contributions and benefits.

8.3 UNEMPLOYMENT AND UNEMPLOYMENT INSURANCE

The basic purpose of this section is to highlight the preceding discussion by concentrating on a specific area of research into the effects of unemployment insurance on the labour market. So far it has been argued not only that changes in UI benefits are of potential importance via the demand and supply schedules of labour but also that changes in UI (and other social welfare) payroll taxes and ceilings have a related role to play. An ideal illustration of the potential importance of this line of argument is provided by those studies that have examined the effect of the benefit replacement ratio, b/y, on the aggregate rate of unemployment.

There has been a major growth of research interest in the relationship between UI and the aggregate rate of unemployment in recent years. The effects of UI on the duration of spells of unemployment (for example, Ehrenberg and Oaxaca, 1976; Hamermesh, 1977; Mortensen, 1977; Nickell, 1979) as well as the related questions of UI effects on labour force participation rates and the frequency of the periods of unemployment (for example Hamermesh, 1980; Spindler and Maki, 1978) have been of particular interest. Much of the literature has developed within a search theoretic framework and has concentrated on the supply side of the labour market. (Two useful reviews can be found in Topel and Welch, 1980, which has a US bias, and Walsh, 1981, with a UK bias.) A popular argument runs as follows. While UI reduces the costs of unemployment, it raises the opportunity cost of searching for a new job relative to undertaking pure leisure. This implies a reduction in search effort or in the 'productivity' of unemployment.[2] The enhanced ability of the individual to prolong job search may also lead to an increase in the minimum, or reservation, wage below which a new job offer may not be accepted. The general tendency is for UI benefit increases to extend spells of unemployment and, possibly, the aggregate rate of unemployment.

In the spirit of this line of reasoning, a number of studies (examples include Spindler and Maki, 1975, 1978; Benjamin and Kochin, 1979) have investigated the effect of b/y on the aggregate average rate of unemployment (u_r). While there are several variations, the main theme of the approach is reasonably accurately represented by the following 'reduced-form' equation:

$$u_r = f(b/y, Q^*) \quad f_1 \geq 0, \; f_2 \leq 0 \tag{8.1}$$

where Q^* is some measure of deviation from trend output. It is incorporated to represent the demand side of the labour market with b/y playing the sort of supply-side role illustrated above. It should be added that, even within a pure supply-side context, arguments can be advanced that question the sign of the partial derivative, f_1 in (8.1). For example, Mortensen (1977) develops the following idea. Many UI schemes require that, in order to qualify for full benefit, a worker must be in the insured labour force for some minimum period. Typically, new entrants to the labour market do not qualify for benefit. Other groups, such as those who have voluntarily quit their job or married women returning to the labour force, also often do not qualify. Given a non-zero expectation of being laid off at some future date, there is an incentive for these groups to reduce their reservation wage by more than if they qualify for benefit. This strategy enables them to find a new job more speedily, thereby increasing their eligibility for benefit when their next layoff occurs. Therefore, whether or not UI is associated with a net rise or fall in u_r depends both on the relative quantitative importance of the 'eligible' and the 'ineligible' groups in a given labour market and on the respective relative elasticity of the reservation wage to the unemployment benefit.

The most serious problem with (8.1) is that, as pointed out by Helliwell, given the dependent variable is u_r, 'one simply does not know how to work back to the micro-behavioural parameters' (Helliwell, 1978, p. 115). Within an *equilibrium* context, suppose we measure u_r as:

$$u_r = (L^P - L^*)/L^P = f(b/y, Q^*) \tag{8.2}$$

where L^* is the market clearing quantity of labour services and L^P is the participating labour force. Following Spindler and Maki (1978), L^P can be regarded as the 'apparent labour supply' and L^* is given by the intersection of the effective demand for and supply of labour services, L^D and L^S respectively. The gap, $L^P - L^*$, represents the amount of structural unemployment, which

> can be either voluntary (as when workers are engaged in searching for another job or enjoying leisure) or involuntary (as when there is a mismatch of worker skill and job requirements, a mismatch of worker and job location, or there is implicit or explicit exclusion of other workers by a favoured group of workers in order to raise the wage of the latter above the market wage). (Spindler and Maki, 1978, p. 149)

The underlying structural equations to the type of reduced-form in (8.1) involve functional specifications of the L's in (8.2) where the L's themselves are functionally related to *both* workers and hours per worker. Relatively simple forms of these functions have been derived by Harrison and Hart (1983a). One of their demand functions is a variant of Model 5.1 that includes b to represent the Feldstein and Baily implicit-contract effect. Elsewhere, Harrison and Hart (1983b) have pointed out a theoretical problem with the benefit replacement ratio and so benefits and wages are entered separately in the L-functions. Their supply and participation functions are based on work by Seater (1977, 1978). We may write these structural equations:

$$L^D = L^D(b, w, z_x, \underline{X}^D) \tag{8.3a}$$

$$L^S = L^S(b, w, \underline{X}^S) \tag{8.3b}$$

$$L^P = L^P(b, w, \underline{X}^P) \tag{8.3c}$$

where w is the real wage and the $\underline{X}$'s are other variables relevant to each function. Now, in order to gain an insight into the specification problem involved in (8.1) we examine Spindler and Maki's (1978) derivation of it. This involves making the simplifying assumptions that hours per worker are fixed and also that the worker demand function is decreasing in real wages.[3] Further, the supply and participation functions are increasing in real wages. Writing (8.3) in terms of workers only, we have:

$$N^D = N^D(b, w, z_x, \underline{X}^D)\, N_1^D \le 0, N_2^D \le 0, N_3^D \le 0 \tag{8.4a}$$

$$N^{S} = N^{S}(b, w, \underline{X}^{S}) N_1^{S} \gtrless 0, N_2^{S} \gtrless 0 \tag{8.4b}$$

$$N^{P} = N^{P}(b, w, \underline{X}^{P}) N_1^{P} \geq 0, N_2^{P} \geq 0. \tag{8.4c}$$

As in section 4.1 suppose that UI contribution rates and benefit rates increase together. Aggregate unemployment, u (equal to the numerator in (8.2), may then increase, decrease or remain unchanged. Two possibilities are illustrated in Figures 8.1(a) and 8.1(b)) where the wage rate is held fixed at $\overline{w}$. In both Case A and Case B, the initial level of unemployment is at u_1, which measures the difference between the initial levels of participation (N_1^P) and market clearing (N_1^D intersects N_1^S). *Ceteris paribus*, both UI benefits and contributions are increased. In both cases, N^P shifts to the right (to N_2^P) given (8.4c). In Case A, both N^D and N^S shift to the left (to N_2^D and N_2^S). This assumes that UI contributions are per-worker costs and thus enter z_x in (8.4a). It also assumes that UI benefits produce supply responses in accord with the standard neoclassical search model; a higher b induces a higher reservation wage and longer search thereby reducing effective labour supply. The net effect under Case A is an unequivocal rise in aggregate unemployment, from u_1 to u_2. In Case B, however, the net effect on unemployment is not so unambiguous. Here both N^D and N^S functions are assumed to shift to the right. The former shift *may* occur if contributions comprise variable NWLCs (which can be assumed to be accommodated by the $\underline{X}^D$ term in (8.4a) and produce the type of worker-for-hours substitution as predicted in Model 5.1 and, possibly, in other models. The latter shift may occur if the

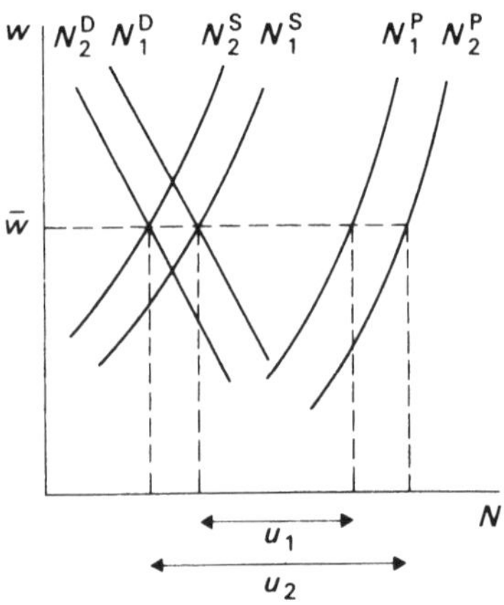

Figure 8.1(a) *Case A*

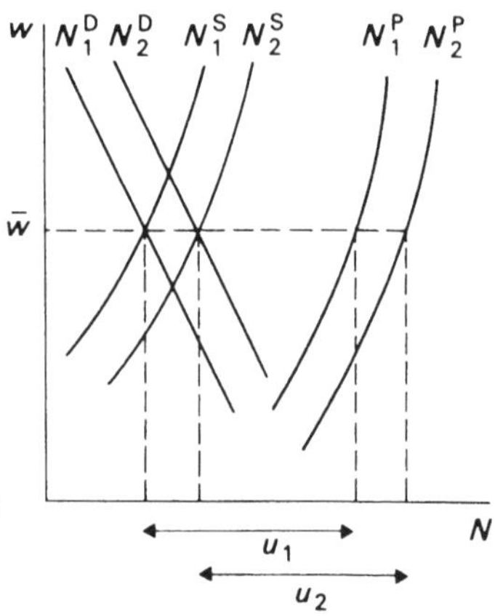

Figure 8.1(b) *Case B*

Mortensen-effect is the dominant supply influence, thereby reducing the average reservation wage and promoting shorter average search spells. Whether or not the new unemployment level, u_2, is greater than, equal to or smaller than u_1 depends on the relative shift of N^P *vis-à-vis* the shift in market clearing positions. Of course, other outcomes are possible but it is clear that, in the absence of a model that describes the complete labour market structure, it is *not* possible to assess the impact of benefit replacement on aggregate unemployment.

Where unemployment contribution rates predominantly constitute a fixed labour cost to the firm, such as in interwar UK or present-day USA, then one is more likely to observe a positive association between u_r and b/y in (8.1). In this instance, Case A in Figure 8.1(a) may serve as a fair approximation to what is taking place. This still leaves the problem, however, of unravelling both the separate influences of benefits and contributions as well as the relative impacts of benefits on demand and supply. Returning to Feldstein's (1978) model, for example, it may well be that the coefficient he obtained on b/y is an overestimate of its true contribution to layoffs given a comparable role played by UI contributions. Harrison and Hart (1983a) have obtained strong empirical evidence that this problem is critical to Benjamin and Kochin's (1979) unemployment equation for interwar Britain. If, on the other hand, contribution rates predominantly constitute a variable labour cost to the firm, as in postwar Europe, then, in the absence of careful modelling, there is reason to be much more sceptical concerning claims that higher unemployment insurance benefits are associated with higher rates of unemployment. Further, this particular problem is magnified if increases in UI contributions occur contemporaneously with increases in other obligatory social welfare payments.

8.4 CONCLUDING REMARKS

Temporary layoffs have played an influential role in the study of several aspects of labour market behaviour in recent years. Practically all the major research effort has been undertaken by US labour market analysts, one of the principal reasons being that significant resort to temporary layoffs is almost exclusively a US phenomenon. FitzRoy and Hart (1983) have attempted to suggest why the difference between the USA and 'elsewhere' has occurred.[4] The work of Clark and Summers (1979) and others has shown that, even within the USA, the quantitative importance of short spells of unemployment (of which temporary layoffs are *one* aspect) is quite small. This present chapter has concentrated on another problem with work in this area.

It argues that reduced-form models of layoffs and unemployment that incorporate unemployment insurance and other benefits as supply-side arguments contain potentially serious specification errors. Social welfare variables also enter the system on the demand side thereby exerting separate, and perhaps opposite, influences on hours of work, employment, layoffs and so on. More work is needed on determining the separate demand-side influences before benefit effects can be adequately assessed.

NOTES

1 In 1978, the ceiling level in most US states rose from $4,200 to $6,000, remaining well below average earnings.
2 Although this conclusion should be tempered. In the first place, in several countries the receipt of UI benefit is conditional on actively undertaking job search. Secondly, offsetting productivity gains may result from better job matching due to longer search time.
3 A complication that we ignore here is that in simple models with fixed NWLCs, such as Model 5.1, worker demand may be *positively* related to the real wage, through the substitution effect. In Models 5.4 and 5.5, on the other hand, a negative relationship between worker demand and the real wage is feasible even through a pure substitution effect.
4 Although FitzRoy and Hart reject the importance of the two most popular explanations for the European dearth of temporary layoffs – short-time working practices and legal obstacles. Apart from the influence of obligatory social welfare contributions, stress is laid on differences in the roles of unions.

REFERENCES

Akerlof, G. A. and B. G. M. Main (1981), 'An experience weighted measure of employment and unemployment durations', *American Economic Review*, 71, 1003–1011.

Baily, M. N. (1977), 'On the theory of layoffs and unemployment', *Econometrica*, 45, 1043–1063.

Bell, D. N. F. (1982), 'Labour utilisation and statutory non-wage costs', *Economica*, 49, 335–343.

Benjamin, D. K. and L. A. Kochin (1979), 'Searching for an explanation of unemployment in inter-war Britain', *Journal of Political Economy*, 87, 441–478.

Brechling, F. (1977), 'The incentive effects of the US unemployment insurance tax', *Research in Labor Economics*, Vol 1, Greenwich, Conn: JAI Press.

Brechling, F. (1981), 'Layoffs and unemployment insurance', in Sherwin Rosen (ed), *Studies in Labour Markets*, National Bureau of Economic Research, Chicago: The University of Chicago Press.

Burdett, K. (1979), 'Unemployment insurance payments as a search subsidy: a theoretical analysis', *Economic Inquiry*, 17, 333–343.

Clark, K. B. and L. H. Summers (1979), 'Labor market dynamics and unemployment: a reconsideration', *Brookings Papers*, Vol. 1, 13–61.

Ehrenberg, R. G. and R. L. Oaxaca (1976), 'Unemployment insurance, duration of unemployment and subsequent wage gain', *American Economic Review*, 66, 754–766.

Feldstein, M. S. (1973), *Lowering the Rate of Unemployment*, US Congress, Joint Economic Committee, Washington DC: US Government Printing Office.

Feldstein, M. S. (1975), 'The importance of temporary layoffs: an empirical analysis', *Brookings Papers*, Vol. 6, 725–744.

Feldstein, M. S. (1976), 'Temporary layoffs in the theory of unemployment', *Journal of Political Economy*, 84, 937–957.

Feldstein, M. S. (1978), 'The effect of unemployment insurance on temporary layoff unemployment', *American Economic Review*, 68, 834–846.

FitzRoy, F. R. and R. A. Hart (1983), 'Hours of work, layoffs and unemployment insurance: theory and practice in an international perspective', Berlin: International Institute of Management, mimeo.

Freeman, R. B. (1980), 'The exit-voice tradeoff in the labor market, unionism, job tenure, quits, and separations', *Quarterly Journal of Economics*, 94, 643–673.

Freeman, R. B. (1981), 'The effect of unionism on fringe benefits', *Industrial and Labor Relations Review*, 34, 489–509.

Freiburghaus, D. (1978), *Dynamik der Arbeitslosigkeit*, Meisenheim: Anton Hain.

Hall, R. E. (1982), 'The importance of lifetime jobs in the US economy', *American Economic Review*, 72, 716–724.

Hamermesh, D. S. (1977), *Jobless Pay and the Economy*, Baltimore, Md: Johns Hopkins University Press.

Hamermesh, D. S. (1980), 'The unemployment insurance and labour supply', *International Economic Review*, 21, 517–527.

Harrison. A. J. and R. A. Hart (1983a), 'A labour market model of unemployment insurance', Berlin: International Institute of Management, mimeo.

Harrison, A. J. and R. A. Hart (1983b), 'Unemployment benefits and labour supply; a note', *Weltwirtschaftliches Archiv*, 119, 169–172.

Hart, R. A. (1982), 'Unemployment insurance and the firm's employment strategy: a European and United States comparison', Kyklos, 35, 648–672.

Helliwell, J. F. (1978), 'Discussion' in H. G. Grubel and M. A. Walker, *Unemployment Insurance: Global Evidence of Its Effects on Unemployment*, Vancouver, BC: The Fraser Institute.

Main, B. G. M. (1982), 'The length of a job in Great Britain', *Economica*, 49, 325–334.

Medoff, J. L. (1979), 'Layoffs and alternatives under trade unions in United States manufacturing', *American Economic Review*, 69, 380–395.

Mortensen, D. T. (1977), 'Unemployment insurance and job search decisions', *Industrial and Labor Relations Review*, 30, 505–517.

Moy, J. and C. Sorrentino (1981), 'Unemployment and layoff practices in 10 countries', *Monthly Labor Review*, 104 (12).

Nickell, S. (1979), 'Education and lifetime patterns of unemployment', *Journal of Political Economy*, 87, 117–132.

Seater, J. J. (1977), 'A unified model of consumption, labor supply and job search', *Journal of Economic Theory*, 14, 349–372.

Seater, J. J. (1978), 'Utility maximisation, aggregate labor force behavior, and the Phillips curve', *Journal of Monetary Economics*, 4, 687–713.

Spindler, Z. A. and D. R. Maki (1975), 'The effect of unemployment compensation on the rate of unemployment in Great Britain', *Oxford Economic Papers*, 27, 440–454.

Spindler, Z. A. and D. R. Maki (1978), 'More on the effects of unemployment compensation on the rate of unemployment in Great Britain', *Oxford Economic Papers*, 31, 147–164.

Topel, R. and F. Welch (1980), 'Unemployment insurance; survey and extensions', *Economica*, 47, 301–322.

Walsh, B. M. (1981), 'Unemployment insurance and the labor market; a review of research in relation to policy', *OECD*, MAS/WPS (81) 1, Paris.

9 Worksharing and Non-Wage Labour Costs

The quantitative importance of obligatory social welfare taxes and their role in influencing firms' employment decisions render them potentially important policy instruments to governments. Of particular interest in this direction is the feasibility of altering the structure of labour costs to the firm in order to encourage 'worksharing'. By worksharing is meant spreading the existing work available among more workers with the aim of reducing the actual, or potential, rate of unemployment. Interest in worksharing has been rekindled in recent times not only because of the severe nature of the current recession but also because of the political climate prevailing in several major OECD countries under which economic solutions have been sought. The picture is one of unemployment rates, accounted for mainly by relatively long spell-lengths, that have reached post-1930s record levels but that have also coincided with the emergence of a more conservative strain of economic and political ideology within government. Towards the late 1970s, inflation, like unemployment, reached record postwar levels and became the preoccupation of finance ministers throughout the OECD. Their weapons have been controlled real money growth, balanced budgets, high interest rate policies – the very antithesis of expenditure-led recovery. The subject of worksharing has returned to the fore because, whatever the existing counter-arguments, it seems to provide a non-expansionist solution, albeit partial, to the problems of high and long-term unemployment.

This chapter is intended to provide a reasonably comprehensive and critical analysis of worksharing possibilities that arise through direct changes in non-wage labour costs or through the indirect effect of NWLCs given changes in other variables. As background, considerable use is made of the comparative static models in Chapter 5 as well as the statistical information in Chapters 2 and 3. The full range of policy options is introduced in section 9.1 with reference to Model 5.2; particular emphasis is given to the possibility of creating worksharing by increasing the average overtime premium rate of pay. Retaining the same model structure, section 9.2 goes on to investigate the attempts by governments to stimulate worksharing by granting wage and non-wage subsidies to firms. Special attention is given to the French so-called 'solidarity contracts'. Some complications concerning the results of the first two sections are discussed in section 9.3. Finally in section 9.4, we return to further problems and repercussions of government changes in social welfare tax rates and ceiling limits.

9.1 FACTOR PRICE CHANGES WITHIN A SIMPLE MODEL

Model 5.2 in Chapter 5 provides an extension to our basic model by explicitly allowing for changes in standard hours as well as the various elements of exogenous fixed and variable NWLCs. Equilibrium solutions are shown in (5.15a) and (5.15b). In this and the following section worksharing is discussed within the context of this one-factor model before dealing, in section 9.3, with the complications associated with the introduction of other endogenous inputs.

Suppose the government introduces a cut in the standard workweek, represented by a fall in h_s in Model 5.2. In the absence of other assumptions this would reduce worksharing and produce a detrimental effect on the size of the workforce. This result is discussed and empirically tested (for the hours equation) in Ehrenberg (1971). The result occurs explicitly because exogenous fixed NWLCs are included in the model; the fall in h_s, *ceteris paribus*, increases the marginal cost of employing a new worker relative to that of extending average hours. One possible offsetting effect, which is not accommodated in Model 5.2, may be that the marginal productivity of hours is enhanced by such a substitution thereby producing beneficial scale effects that may enhance employment prospects in the longer term. For example, if one accepts Feldstein's (1967) arguments of increasing returns to hours, due in part to an unproductive use of h_s (set-up time, tea-breaks, union meetings, etc.), then an increased use of overtime, as implied by the model here, may have beneficial productivity effects. However, as discussed in section 6.6.(i), it is difficult to be other than sceptical about this interpretation of returns to hours, and the predicted adverse employment effects of a reduction in h_s cannot be dismissed lightly. An interesting result is that worksharing is encouraged (i.e. a substitution of N for h) by a *rise* in the standard wage, w_s. This would seem to give some support for general union unwillingness to offset reductions in h_s by 'compensating' reductions in w_s. A clear example of this reluctance in the case of European trade unions can be found in the recent pronouncements of their representative body, the European Trade Union Institute (1979; see, in particular, part II, pp 12–30, of this report). It should be emphasised that, as with the other results discussed in this section, this analysis ignores scale effects (which would be adverse if w_s rises) as well as capital and productivity substitution possibilities.

Changes in the overtime premium, α, are of most interest to North American economies. Two legislative measures were introduced in the USA in the 1930s that imposed constraints on α. Under the Fair Labor Standards Act employers are required to pay premium rates of time-and-a-half for hours worked in excess of a standard forty-hour week. The Walsh-Healy Public Contract Act imposed such overtime premiums on work in excess of eight hours in one day. Ehrenberg (1971) attempts to quantify the employment implications of increasing these premium payments from 150 to 200 per cent given *ceteris paribus* assumptions. Ehrenberg is interested particularly in changes in the overtime wage rate *relative* to weekly fixed NWLCs per worker. He represents this by the variable z/w_p (where numerator and denominator are defined in (5.4) and (5.7), respectively) in a regression equation with annual overtime hours as dependent variable. The theoretical rationale behind the use of this ratio is the same as that given for z_x/v in Model 5.1 and, as in equation (5.14b), it is predicted to have a positive influence on overtime hours. His estimates indicate that the employment increases induced by this change in the premium would range between 1 per cent and 3 per cent with a fair degree of stability across the sixteen two-digit manufacturing industries in his 1966 sample. The overall absolute increase in employment in these industries is estimated to be 218,000 jobs from an existing base of 3,616,000. Analogous results are obtained for the non-manufacturing sector. Similar estimates for Canadian manufacturing industry (Laudadio and Percy, 1973) suggest that an identical increase in the premium rate would increase employment by 1.5 per cent.

In order to obtain these employment estimates, the critical assumption is made that the fall in overtime hours due to the rise in premium payments (which, incidentally, are estimated to be a substantial proportion of the existing overtime hours worked) would be totally compensated for by a rise in manhours comprising new employees each working 2,000 hours per year. A consideration of various offsetting effects, however, leads Ehrenberg to be extremely cautious over his estimates of induced employment. Such effects include, on the demand side, capital for labour substitution given the relative price increase of the latter factor and, on the supply side, an hours substitution effect as workers increase their demand for overtime due to the higher premium payments.

A follow-up study by Ehrenberg and Schumann (1982) produces, if anything, even more guarded conclusions. Using cross-sectional samples of manufacturing and non-manufacturing establishments for 1976, the ratio z/w_p is again found to enter the overtime (log-linear) equation with a significant positive coefficient. When the two components of the ratio are entered separately, however, only the non-manufacturing equations produce significant results that display a correct sign on each variable *and* consistency with the ratio specification. The upper-bound employment gain is estimated to be (for different specifications) 1.0–2.3 per cent. In the manufacturing equations, the separate influence of the overtime premium is found to be insignificant. The authors further allow for the possibility that z/w_p is simultaneously determined by producing two-stage least squares estimates. Simultaneity may arise through the increase in the overtime premium inducing the firm to lower fringes so as to reduce labour costs. While, on the one hand, these estimates indicate larger employment-inducing effects, they also suggest, on the other, that increases in overtime reduce the ratio z/w_p. Since it is difficult to rationalise this latter result, the authors treat the two-stage least squares approach with some scepticism. At least the view may be taken that the non-manufacturing results may encourage, perhaps selective, legislative measures in this direction. The authors more or less reject such a recommendation after careful consideration of a number of other factors that combine to reduce their 'maximum possible' employment estimates. These include the offsetting effects of (i) capital substitution given higher labour costs (ii) negative scale effects due to forward shifting, (iii) indivisibilities in the production process preventing the conversion of fewer overtime hours into more jobs, and (iv) skill mismatch between those who experience reduced overtime and those who are unemployed.

From (5.15a) and (5.15b) we note that a rise in the social welfare contribution tax rate, β, will lead to greater worksharing. Thus, pressure on governments by employers' associations and other groups to lower such contributions *may not* have beneficial employment effects. Of course, this conclusion overlooks capital–labour substitution and other possibilities that are discussed below.

Finally, although we do not model most of the facets connected with the variables associated with the effects on worksharing of early retirement, such as seniority-based payments systems and the relative productivity of older workers, one pertinent point can be noted. In so far as an early retirement scheme forces an employer to release a worker earlier than would have been the case without the scheme, this may well cause an increase in the rate, r, at which fixed investments are discounted, thereby producing a detrimental effect on worksharing (see again, equations (5.15a) and (5.15b)).

9.2 WAGE AND NON-WAGE SUBSIDIES

Changes in some of the variables in equations (5.15a) and (5.15b) may occur due to direct government subsidies. There are well-known examples of subsidies that reduce both per-worker and variable labour costs to the firm. Examples of the former type include reductions of social welfare contributions for workers with earnings above ceiling-limits ($\bar{z}_x$ reduced), direct subsidies to training investment and, simply, lump-sum payments to each employee ($\bar{z}_x$ reduced)). Direct wage subsidies (w_s reduced) and variable social welfare cost subsidies (β reduced) provide obvious examples of the latter type.

Subsidies with respect to the whole of a firm's payroll arise, usually, from selective industrial economic policies. Almost invariably, they are paid to firms within industries and/or within geographical regions that are in relative structural decline. The main motive behind the subsidies is to produce beneficial *scale effects*. The cost subsidy may reduce relative prices and increase demand for the firm's final product, which in turn feeds back to produce improved employment (and capital investment) prospects. The potential impact of the scale effects depends on two factors: first, the relative importance of labour payments within the firm's total cost structure; secondly, the size of the firm's output elasticity of demand.

As is readily apparent from the type of analysis underlying the outcomes of equations (5.15a) and (5.15b), subsidies to labour costs will also produce *substitution effects* within labour services and these provide real complications in assessing a given subsidy's net impact. In investigating substitution effects, we analyse a special type of subsidy programme that seems to be gaining increasing interest as a policy instrument.

The policy initiatives of interest in this section are those that make labour cost subsidies *conditional* on the firm increasing its number of workers beyond those on the existing payroll. One such scheme, the US New Jobs Tax Credit of 1977, has been quite fully discussed in the literature (see, for example, Eisner, 1978). Here we concentrate on the latest major example of this approach, which forms part of the French so-called 'solidarity contracts'. Since 1 February 1982, France has had a standard thirty-nine-hour week. A French employer may receive state subsidies with respect to newly hired employees if he/she signs a contract with the Labour Ministry along the following lines. The employer must undertake to schedule a cut in the standard work week by at least a further two hours per week, resulting in a basic working week of at most thirty-seven hours (by 1 January 1983) or thirty-six hours (by 1 September 1983). The reductions may cover all or part of the workforce. State subsidies will then be granted with respect to new recruits,[1] over and above the existing workforce, employed as a result of the working time reductions. The subsidy takes the form of a partial or total exemption of the employer from social welfare payments with respect to the new recruits.[2] Therefore, under this scheme, the subsidy is dependent upon the employer fulfilling two basic conditions: first, reducing standard working hours below the existing level and, secondly, increasing the existing workforce. In order to analyse the outcome within our framework, we shall separate the procedure into two distinct parts. To start with, it is assumed that the subsidy is conditional *only* on increasing the existing workforce. This has the advantage of enabling us both to investigate other, simpler schemes, such as the aforementioned US Act, as well as to clarify the outcome for the more complicated French scheme. The second stage, therefore, consists of adding the condition that standard hours should also be reduced. Further, the model background adopted in the previous section is still considered to pertain throughout.

Thus, suppose the government offers a labour cost subsidy to new recruits who are employed *over and above* the firm's existing workforce. For completeness, consideration is given to the possibility that the subsidy may be paid with respect to wages *or* social welfare contributions. The latter subsidy may, therefore, relate to variable or fixed labour costs. The subsidies affect existing labour cost variables in the following manner:

$$\left.\begin{aligned} w_s^s &= (1-\mu_1)w_s && (9.1a)\\ w_n^s &= \beta(1-\mu_2)w_s(1+\alpha) && (9.1b)\\ z_x^s &= (1-\mu_3)z_x && (9.1c)\end{aligned}\right\}\quad 0 \le \mu_i < 1, N > N_0$$

where 's' superscript denotes a subsidised wage and non-wage, μ_i is the rate of subsidy[3] and N_0 is the pre-subsidy size of the firm's workforce.

Given the high social welfare contribution ceilings in France, the typical firm entering into the solidarity contract described above will receive a subsidised non-wage, w_n^s as in (9.1b). If payment is *unconditional* on a standard hours reduction, then the following outcome, illustrated with the aid of Figure 9.1, would be expected. (More technical details relating to Figure 9.1 are given in an Appendix to this chapter.) Suppose that, pre-subsidy, the firm is in equilibrium, employing N_0h_0 manhours.[4] Graphically, this is illustrated in Figure 9.1 as the point where the firm's cost curve, C_0C_0 is tangential to the isoemployment locus, LL, at point X. If, now, the government provides a subsidy to the firm's variable social welfare payments conditional on the firm extending its workforce beyond N_0, then this will alter the firm's cost schedule. In fact, at existing total labour costs, the cost function above N_0 will be a steeper (convex) curve as represented by XC_1. Assuming the existence of conditions to achieve a minimum, there is a cost curve that satisfies the budget constraint and that

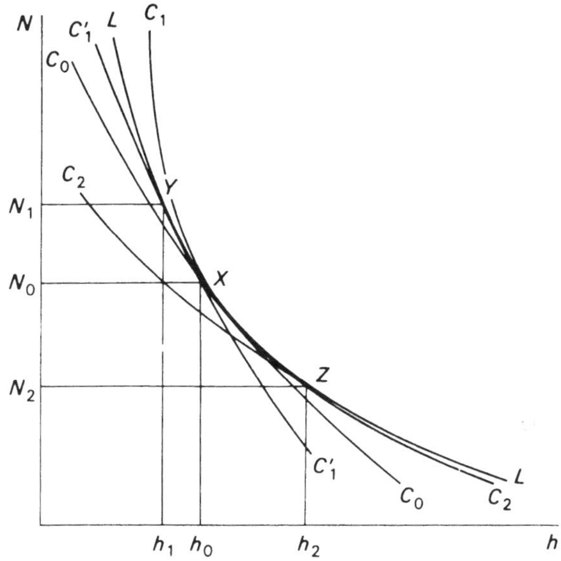

Figure 9.1

represents total labour costs less than pre-subsidy costs. Such a curve is represented by $C_1'C_1'$, which is tangential to LL at point Y. The firm will increase its workforce by amount N_1-N_0 and reduce its hours per worker by amount h_0-h_1.

Moreover (as is shown in the Appendix), irrespective of whether the subsidy takes the form w_n^s or w_s^s or z_x^s in (9.1), this basic outcome remains unaltered. A subsidy to the firm's direct or per capita labour costs with respect to new workers hired over and above existing (equilibrium) numbers will induce the firm to substitute more workers for fewer hours per worker. Of course, the subsidy will also produce scale effects, which may enhance the total new-worker employment effect while also restoring – partially or completely or more than completely – the fall-off in average working hours.

Returning specifically to the French solidarity contract, the subsidy is also conditional on a prior reduction in standard hours. Unfortunately, this second condition renders the final outcome ambiguous. Consider the decision problem of a French firm that has to assess whether or not it will sign a contract under these terms. In the first place, the required reduction in standard hours would, following the analysis of the previous section, produce a substitution of more hours per worker for fewer hours. This is shown graphically in Figure 9.1 by a change in the slope of the cost curve from C_0C_0 to C_2C_2, producing N_2h_2 at point Z equilibrium combination of manhours.[5] As before, the subsidy per new hire will change the slope of C_2C_2 above N_0. However, since C_2C_2 lies *inside LL* at N_0, whether or not the post-subsidy cost curve above N_0 crosses the unchanged isoemployment locus is purely an empirical question. A particular outcome depends on the firm's perceived size of the marginal worker cost increases due to the fall in h_s relative to the marginal worker cost decrease due to the subsidy. The unavoidable conclusion is that, for some potential firm participants, the standard hours' clause in the contract would discourage employment expansion and a take-up of the subsidy. Indeed, the conclusion would appear to be borne out by evidence of the actual performance of this type of French solidarity contract. At the end of 1982, the scheme was radically revised; of the contracts signed up until that time, about 95 per cent dealt with early retirement options and only around 5 per cent contained provision for reducing working time and increasing employment (creating, in a macro context, extremely few new jobs).

It is of interest to mention the relative merits of *general* as opposed to *marginal* wage and non-wage subsidies within the context of the present model structure. By 'general' is meant a subsidy that applies to all the firm's existing workforce as well as its potential future net additions. By 'marginal' is meant the kind of subsidy discussed above. Both types of subsidy would be expected to exhibit beneficial scale effects on final product prices. Presumably, within a longer-term context, both types of subsidy may encourage the firm to substitute workers for capital. However, differences are likely to emerge with respect to worker–hours substitution. While *all* the marginal subsidies will produce worker-for-hours substitution, only a general subsidy on *fixed* worker costs will produce a comparable result. Following the results of the previous section, a general subsidy on variable labour costs will produce substitution of hours for workers, thereby offsetting beneficial employment scale effects. Moreover, since for most firms social welfare payments constitute variable labour costs, then this offsetting substitution possibility is likely to be the most usually observed outcome. Therefore, the approach here lends support to Layard and Nickell (1980) who, within the context of a much fuller macroeconomic model, argue for the advantages of marginal as opposed to general subsidies as a means of creating new jobs.

9.3 COMPLICATING FACTORS

The outcomes of initiatives to encourage worksharing by reducing obligatory non-wage labour costs or by selective wage and non-wage subsidies are rendered far less certain when wider economic issues are considered. The strength of the Ehrenberg and Schumann (1982) approach is their careful consideration of a number of possibilities that may serve to reduce the job-creating impact of increased overtime premiums. Indeed, their wider evaluation leads them to reject legislative measures *despite* obtaining encouraging econometric results (at least for non-manufacturing). One additional issue of interest to them is the firm's wage elasticity of the demand for labour. If this is found to be completely inelastic then, *ceteris paribus*, a reduction in overtime would be completely converted into new jobs. As the authors acknowledge (with reference to other researchers' estimates), this is unlikely to be the case and the increase in labour costs would be expected to produce substitution and scale effects that would serve to offset the new job potential. The most obvious substitution effect is a move by the firm towards a more capital-intensive means of production. Model 5.4 helps to illustrate how allowing for the capital stock as a variable factor input results in confounding employment outcomes given changes in factor prices. The wage elasticity estimates adopted by Ehrenberg and Schumann tend to suggest that the capital substitution effect may not be large in their particular study but wherever worksharing policy objectives pertain this problem remains as an open empirical question.

Of course, the two-factor input dimension helps to confound the employment effects not only of policies designed to subsidise wages and non-wages but also of those that subsidise capital. A popular argument among European 'policy makers' in recent years is that there has been a trend towards subsidising capital investment relative to labour costs that has led to the substitution of capital for labour thereby exacerbating adverse employment trends. The following European Economic Community summary of a group of independent experts crystallises this sentiment:

> The granting of interest rate subsidies, tax relief in respect of depreciation, and investment aids (regional or others) lowers the cost of using capital. Furthermore, the use of wages as the base for social security contributions and certain parafiscal charges lead to changes in the parameters within which the employer makes his calculations and tends to accelerate the substitution of capital for labour. (Commission of the European Communities, 1976, p. 50)

Thus it is suggested that subsidies to capital, such as through policies designed to lower interest rates (i.e. π in (5.9)) or depreciation costs (δ in (5.9)), combined with the burden of wage-related social welfare contributions, have produced a climate that has favoured, at the margin, more and/or better vintage machines combined with fewer workers. These outcomes, while possible, are by no means certain; the solutions in (5.20) and (5.21) reveal that opposite outcomes are feasible. Similar conclusions hold if one allows for endogenous changes in worker productivity, as in Model 5.5.

9.4 CHANGES IN SOCIAL WELFARE TAX RATES AND CEILINGS

In Table 2.8, we present estimates of the ratio of fixed to variable labour costs for the UK and USA between 1973 and 1981. These indicate ratios in the region of 0.17– 0.26 in the respective countries. The cross-sectional breakdown of this ratio by UK industries in Table 2.9 and its positive correlation with weekly overtime hours per worker is, at least, suggestive of the possibility that reductions in the ratio may help towards shortening average working hours and creating more jobs. Ehrenberg and Schumann in their overtime study (1982) investigate the worksharing consequences of changing one element in the ratio through a measure that has perhaps limited possibilities outside the USA.[6] There are other elements in the ratio and, at first glance, it would appear that there is considerable further scope for governments to reduce the ratio by other means in the pursuit of the same basic policy goal. As is by now well established, one limiting factor on the room for manoeuvre is the fact that at least half of NWLCs (see Table 2.2) result from some degree of choice exercised by the firm. Returning to Table 2.9, the industrial labour cost ratios also display strong positive correlations with industrial skill ratios, which one might expect given the importance of endogenous NWLCs. However, the great bulk of exogenous NWLCs consists of statutory social welfare contributions, which are clearly more amenable to policy initiatives given that their parameters are set by governments.

Governments can make significant alterations to the ratio through tax-rate and/or wage–ceiling[7] changes to social welfare contributions. Since, as emphasised in the previous chapter, the majority of workers in most countries receive wages that lie below ceiling limits, a reduction in the ratio would predominantly involve increasing social welfare taxes. This approach is, of course, conceptually close to increases in the minimum overtime premium and it is open to the same set of doubts about its net effectiveness. For example, it is likely to precipitate offsetting scale effects and capital–productivity substitution effects as well as some degree of compensating wage reactions by the firm. On the other hand, it should be noted that *reductions* in social welfare taxes, a policy measure that appears to be gaining considerable support by governments in Europe, may produce longer-term beneficial scale and factor substitution responses by firms *but also* possible unfavourable short-run effects on worksharing.

Changes in wage ceilings in order to reduce the ratio may appear to involve even more uncertain outcomes. Consider a marginal increase in the ceiling limit. Here, the variable-cost rises associated with those wages that switch from above to below ceiling limits will be partially, exactly or more than offset by the fixed-cost rises associated with those workers whose wages remain above the new ceiling. The net effect of a marginal ceiling change is unclear.[8] However, what if ceilings were removed completely, with the limit effectively infinity? In fact, several countries have no ceiling limits on parts or all of their social welfare taxes; Finland, Italy and Japan provide three examples. This would produce a once-for-all reduction in fixed labour costs with beneficial worksharing implications through substitution. Once again, there may be adverse scale and factor substitution effects but, for many firms, these would be less serious than tax increases, since removing ceilings would increase costs only for that fraction of workers with wages above ceiling limits.

The main problems with policies designed significantly to increase (or completely remove) wage ceilings concern distributional effects on employment. As is suggested in Tables 2.6 and 2.7, the sizes of the ratios of ceiling levels to average wages are negatively related to skill. For obvious reasons, ceiling/wage ratios are also affected by whether or not a given workforce is predominantly male or female. At one end of the spectrum, in the FRG, the ceilings for female blue-collar workers are roughly twice average wages, which is tantamount to no ceiling limit. At the other end, male white-collar workers have significantly lower ratios, with one major case (health insurance) of the ceiling being below average wages. Three points now arise. First, the proportions of obligatory social welfare costs to total labour costs are highest among manual and less skilled workers (see Table 3.4) and yet these are the very groups whose associated fixed costs would be *unaffected* by ceiling changes. Secondly, and of somewhat more importance, the potential of wage-ceiling increases to create new jobs among those groups whose fixed costs would be reduced may be frustrated by supply constraints since their skills might not be matched by the skills of the unemployed.[9] Equivalently, in the Ehrenberg and Schumann study, skill mismatches between those working overtime and the unemployed are viewed as a serious impediment to job creation through overtime reductions. Thirdly, where a firm's capital and organisational structure require a degree of fixed proportionality among skill groups then a rise in the ceiling that reduces fixed costs for some groups and not others (see the examples in section 5.3) may lead to potentially significant adjustment costs, which would tend to offset any worksharing impact.

Another aspect of worksharing in relation to social welfare wage ceilings has been raised by Meltz *et al.* (1981). This concerns job sharing and, more specifically, the case of a full-time job being split into two or more part-time segments. There are many initiatives in this direction throughout the OECD, especially in connection with phased retirement. If the full-time job slot is a relatively highly paid one with a remuneration above the ruling wage ceilings, then the creation of part-time units is likely to result in a net increase in labour costs equivalent to the social welfare taxes multiplied by the difference between the full-time wage level and the ceiling limit. While there is a disincentive scale effect here, emphasised by Meltz *et al.*, there is also a possible beneficial substitution effect given a reduction in labour fixity.

Finally, it should be emphasised that while we have concentrated in this chapter on assessing the effects of changes in relative factor prices on worksharing, the results can be generalised to worksharing initiatives that involve crude attempts to impose working time limits directly. Obvious examples would include reductions in the length of the standard working week or limitations on the number of per capita overtime hours worked per period of time. Such measures themselves alter the structure of relative prices and, therefore, lead implicitly to the questions raised here.

APPENDIX

The problem discussed in section 9.2 is similar to that examined in Rosen (1978). To avoid unnecessary detail, the developments are simplified here by not distinguishing between standard and overtime hours or among the three types of variable labour cost. Consider first the case of a variable labour cost subsidy, ϕ, paid if the firm employs more than its existing (equilibrium) workforce, which is at N_0 (see Figure 9.1). The effect of this type of subsidy is equivalent to the effects of the subsidies, μ_1 and μ_2 represented in (9.1a) and (9.1b) of the main text. In the post-subsidy period, the firm is faced by one of two possible cost functions:

$$C = z_x N + vNh \qquad N \leq N_0 \quad \text{(A9.1)}$$

$$C = z_x N_0 + z_x(N - N_0) + vN_0 h + v(1 - \phi)h(N - N_0) \quad N > N_0. \quad \text{(A9.2)}$$

In the case of (A9.2), for given C, we obtain:

$$\frac{dN}{dh} = \frac{-N_0 z_x v\phi - vC(1-\phi)}{[z_x + vh(1-\phi)]^2} < 0. \tag{A9.3}$$

Note, as $\phi \to 0$ in (A9.3), then:

$$\frac{dN}{dh} \to \frac{-vC}{[z_x + vh]^2} = \frac{-vN^2}{C} < 0. \tag{A9.4}$$

Expression (A9.4) corresponds to the slope of the initial, pre-subsidy cost curve C_0C_0 in Figure 9.1, while expression (A9.3) corresponds to the slope of the post-subsidy curve, XC_1, for $N > N_0$. For this latter curve, note further that:

$$\frac{d^2N}{dh^2} = \frac{-[2v^2h(1-\phi)^2 + 2z_x v(1-\phi)][-N_0 z_x v\phi - vC(1-\phi)]}{[z_x + vh(1-\phi)]^4} > 0. \tag{A9.5}$$

Thus, given (A9.3) and (A9.5), XC_1, like C_0C_0, is convex, a result that contrasts to Rosen (1978), who claims that the post-subsidy cost curve is concave. In order to evaluate the steepness of XC_1 relative to C_0C_0, (A9.3) is differentiated with respect to the subsidy parameter ϕ. Evaluating the differential at $N = N_0$, for given C, N and h, we obtain after some manipulation:

$$\frac{\partial}{\partial\phi}\left(\frac{dN}{dh}\right) = \frac{-[Cv^3h^2(1-\phi)^2 + N_0 z_x v^3 h^2(1-\phi)^2 + 2N_0 z_x v^3 h^2 \phi(1-\phi) + N_0 z_x^2 v^2 h]}{[z_x + vh(1-\phi)]^4} < 0. \tag{A9.6}$$

So that, in the neighbourhood of N_0, XC_1 is steeper than C_0C_0.

Consider next the effects of a fixed labour cost subsidy, ψ (equivalent to μ_3 in (9.1c)). The post-subsidy cost function for $N > N_0$ is given by:

$$C = z_x N_0 + z_x(1-\psi)(N - N_0) + vN_0h + vh(N - N_0) \quad N > N_0. \tag{A9.7}$$

For given C, we have:

$$\frac{dN}{dh} = \frac{-v[C - N_0 z_x \psi]}{[z_x(1-\psi) + vh]^2} \tag{A9.8}$$

which reduces to (A9.4) as $\psi \to 0$. Twice differentiating N with respect to h in (A9.7) gives $\mathrm{d}^2N/\mathrm{d}h^2 > 0$ and differentiating (A9.8), given N and h, with respect to ψ yields $\partial(\mathrm{d}N/\mathrm{d}h)/\partial\psi < 0$. Thus, the effects of a fixed labour cost subsidy are strictly equivalent to those of a variable cost subsidy.

NOTES

1 The employer, as a priority, is required to recruit, on standard, open-ended contracts, job seekers who are either young people under 26 years, women who head one-parent families or unemployed persons in receipt of unemployment benefits or whose entitlement to such benefits has just ended.

2 If the reductions in standard hours are two–three hours, then the employer will receive a 75 per cent exemption from contributions payable for one year, followed by a 50 per cent exemption for the next year, in respect of each new recruit. For reductions of three or more hours, the equivalent reductions are 100 per cent and 75 per cent respectively.

3 Note that, unlike the wage variables in (9.1a) and (9.1b), the subsidy, μ_3 in (9.1c), is not paid on all z_x. Some elements of exogenous fixed non-wage costs are items other than social welfare payments. However, to avoid tedious complication, we do not attempt to disaggregate z_x further; clearly the greater the number of non-subsidised elements, the smaller the value of μ_3 within the total expression.

4 Since we are assuming that the firm is operating in the overtime region, the discontinuity in the isocost curve at h_s is not represented.

5 Writing the cost function $C = z_x + w_s(1+\beta)Nh_s + \alpha w_s(1+\beta)N(h-h_s)$ where (from (5.4) and (5.5)) $z_x = \bar{z}_x + (q+r)\bar{z}_x$, we obtain, for given C:

$$\frac{\mathrm{d}N}{\mathrm{d}h} = \frac{-\alpha w_s(1+\beta)N^2}{C} < 0$$

and so, for given N and h:

$$\frac{\partial(\mathrm{d}N/\mathrm{d}h)}{\partial h_s} = \frac{\alpha w_s(1+\beta)N^2[w_s(1+\beta)N(1-\alpha)]}{C^2} < 0;$$

i.e. a *ceteris paribus* fall in h_s will algebraically increase the slope of C_0C_0.

6 In European countries, while there are some restrictions on overtime working, there are no comparable minimum premium pay standards to the USA. In the medium term, there would seem to be little scope in Europe for creating worksharing along the lines studied by Ehrenberg and Schumann (1982).

7 Although, from the information provided in Chapter 2 and its Appendix, there is relatively little scope for further increases in the ratios of tax ceiling levels to average wages, some recent changes have been substantial. For example, Ehrenberg and Schumann (1982) quote figures that show that the US ratios under the OASDHI system rose between 1960 and 1978 to the extent that the fraction of total covered employees with wages at or above the ceiling fell from 0.28 at the start to 0.10 at

the end of the period. This reduced by over 50 per cent the fraction of employees for whom the OASDHI tax constituted a recurring fixed NWLC. Further, although exceptional by European standards, the Belgian ceiling rose in 1982 from roughly equal to average wages to double average wages.

8 In many countries the ceilings are increased each year in nominal terms, but this is usually undertaken to keep pace with wage inflation and so the likely employment effects are negligible.

9 Similar distributional problems may be expected to occur in relation to the impacts of ceiling (and tax) changes disaggregated by type of industry. Any worksharing reactions that do take place are likely to be felt in those industries where labour costs in general, and NWLCs in particular, comprise a high proportion of net value added. As illustrated in Table 3.3, there are wide divergencies in this respect among industries. The problem of job matching between new vacancies and the unemployed will also arise in this dimension.

REFERENCES

Commission of the European Communities (1976), *Outlook for Employment in the European Community to 1980*, Brussels: Directorate-General for Social Affairs.

Ehrenberg, R. G. (1971), *Fringe Benefits and Overtime Behavior*, Massachusetts DC: Heath & Co.

Ehrenberg, R. G. and P. L. Schumann (1982), *Longer Hours or More Jobs?* Cornell Studies in Industrial and Labor Relations No. 22 New York: Cornell University.

Eisner, R. (1978), 'Employment taxes and subsidies', in *Work Time and Employment*, Washington DC: National Commission for Manpower Policy.

European Trade Union Institute (1979), *Reduction of Working Hours in Western Europe*, Brussels: Günter Köpke.

Feldstein, M. S. (1967), 'Specification of the labour input in the aggregate production function', *Review of Economic Studies*, 34, 375–386.

Laudadio, L. and M. Percy, (1973), 'Some evidence of the impact of non-wage labour cost on overtime work and environment, *Industrial Relations/Industrielles*, 28, 397–403.

Layard, P. R. G. and S. J. Nickell (1980), 'The case for subsidising extra jobs', *Economic Journal*, 90, 51–73.

Meltz, N. M., F. Reid and G. S. Schwartz (1981), *Sharing the Work*, Toronto: University of Toronto Press.

Rosen, S. (1978), 'The supply of work schedules and employment', in *Work Time and Employment*, Washington, DC: National Commission for Manpower Policy.

10 Fringe Benefit Payments

With the exception of the FRG, non-obligatory social welfare contributions in Table 3.1 exhibit among the highest proportions of total non-wage labour costs and the highest growth rates in these proportions. As can be seen from Table A2.6, this category is almost entirely composed of various types of compensation in the form of fringe benefits. Moreover, although it is difficult to obtain precise estimates, there is little doubt that a large proportion (in excess of 60 per cent) of the fringes contain elements of deferred compensation. Here would be included health and life insurance cover and pension provision as well as elements of vacation pay from the category 'payments for days not worked'. The growing importance of fringes within total worker compensation and, in particular, the union/non-union fringe differential have attracted much recent interest and it is the purpose of this chapter to review aspects of the literature within the context of some of these developments.

Sections 10.1, 10.2 and 10.3 discuss three broad approaches to tackling the question of why firms pay fringes. These are, respectively, the human capital, 'agency' and median voter models. A problem of distinguishing among the models is raised in section 10.4. Finally, in section 10.5, a brief comment is made on the recent literature dealing with the relationship between minimum wages and fringe benefits.

10.1 THE HUMAN CAPITAL RATIONALE

Human capital theorists (in particular, see Becker, 1964) tend to argue that firms employing workers with high levels of specific investments, acquired through training and on the job, find it to their advantage to share the quasi-rent from the associated productivity gains in the form of deferred fringe benefit compensation. This reduces the frequency of quits, thereby reducing the user costs of labour (see expression (5.5)). While persuasive up to a point, this argument by itself suffers from several shortcomings.

Labour turnover in general (i.e. both quits and layoffs) is negatively correlated with the firm's level of specific human capital investment (see Parsons, 1972). The higher such investment then the more expensive are worker–job separations. Given a job quit, the firm stands to lose its share of the quasi-rent as represented by the difference between the worker's marginal value product and the wage. On the other hand, a worker who is laid off loses his/her share of the quasi-rent as represented by the wage premium, or the difference between the current and opportunity wages. In other words, both sides have a strong interest in forming a long-term relationship given high specific investments *per se* that render further incentives superfluous.

It might be argued, however, that if deferred fringes involve no special additional costs compared to other forms of labour remuneration, then their attribute as a second line of defence against premature separation provides the firm with a marginal incentive to pay them. Without further arguments from outside a human capital framework, this position is somewhat difficult to defend. At least four strong reasons can be advanced to support the contention that deferred fringes are a relatively costly form of worker compensation.

In the first place, they represent future commitments by the firm in much the same way as do seniority wages in Okun's toll model. When faced with unanticipated product demand falls, the firm will be reluctant to renege on such commitments since the resulting 'bad faith' may stimulate above-normal future quits and/or adverse collective worker reaction. Unfulfilled fringe benefit expectations may have particularly serious consequences since, within the firm itself, fringe growth paths, such as holiday entitlements, are often more 'visible' than wage paths. In summary, deferred fringes may serve to limit the firm's ability to respond to economic fluctuations through variations in labour compensation.

Secondly, by their very design, the cost of certain types of deferred fringe is likely to increase in absolute terms and as a proportion of a worker's total labour cost both with the age of an employee and with years of service. This is illustrated in some detail by Barnow and Ehrenberg (1979) in the case of the most common type of private pension scheme, the so-called 'defined pension plan', which guarantees the worker a specified amount of pension upon retirement. In order to offset these rising costs, firms may be tempted to achieve compensating wage differentials and/or higher turnover rates among older workers. Again, however, anticipation of such strategies by the workforce may provoke costly quits or resistance. Of course, these types of problem are reduced if both costs *and* productivity are rising, relative to length of service. Indeed, in the typical human capital story, accumulated on-the-job specific human capital will produce such a productivity response, and so the deferred fringe may simply reflect one of the means of paying the worker's share of the quasi-rent.

A third, and highly related, problem therefore arises if it is found to be the case that this productivity pattern does *not* hold. There is increasing evidence that productivity grows far less than proportionately to earnings by length of service. Perhaps the best example to date is provided by Medoff and Abraham (1980) who study the earnings and productivity profiles by length of service of white-collar employees within certain grade levels in two large US corporations. They find either no association or a *negative* association between experience and relative performance, in sharp contrast to a strong positive association between experience and relative earnings.

Fourthly, the proportional costs to the firm of administering fringe payments, which can involve relatively complicated rules and conditions, are likely to be considerably in excess of those associated with wages.

Thus, at least within the standard Oi/Becker framework, the view that deferred fringe benefit payments act as protection investments (see Chapter 4) against future losses of specific human capital has only a limited appeal. Not only are labour units endowed with relatively high specific investments less likely *per se* to be involved in quits/layoffs but also deferred fringes provide a relatively costly form of discouraging quits even further.

A somewhat stronger human capital argument, which provides a sounder rationale for recourse to deferred fringe compensation, is achieved by embracing Hashimoto's (1981) concepts of uncertainty on the part of the firm and its workforce over the returns to specific investments (see Chapters 4 and 7). Given high and asymmetrical information costs of reaching reliable estimates of the returns, both sides may seek to minimise the uncertainty over their own and, especially, the other party's estimates by agreeing to deferred fringes as an integral part of a quasi long-term contract. Such an agreement provides a signal from one side to the other of serious long-term commitments despite the possibilities of future disappointments over actual as compared to expected returns. They would optimise their joint position by choosing a proportion of deferred payments within total compensation the marginal cost of which is equal to the marginal cost of improving their mutually agreed information about expected returns. While this line of reasoning helps to explain the adoption of relatively costly deferred fringes, it falls well short of squaring with the sort of findings presented by Medoff and Abraham. There is little doubt that if the association between workers' age and performance profiles is weak then other major reasons for fringe payments that lie outside the human capital framework should be sought.

10.2 LAZEAR'S AGENCY MODEL

Building on the so-called 'agency' literature (see Becker and Stigler, 1974), Lazear (1981) has developed a model in which the firm's optimal age–earnings strategy is to pay workers less than their marginal value product in their early years with the firm and more in their later years. Paying senior workers relatively high wages acts as an incentive to increase work effort among junior colleagues who are aspiring to their positions. The incentive arises primarily because the costs to workers of delayed promotion or dismissal as a result of relatively poor work performance are higher than with other types of wage agreement. This would certainly be the case compared to a spot wage contract that constantly equates the wage with the marginal product or a quasi long-term contract under the human capital approach whereby the wage lies between the opportunity wage and the marginal product. Given that the payment of deferred fringes may be one of the adopted mechanisms of giving relatively high compensation to senior workers, this approach perhaps provides a better rationale for the payment of fringes from the firm's perspective. At least it fits better with the Medoff and Abraham findings. It also provides a possible mechanism by which fringes may directly influence worker productivity, thus supporting the construction of the productivity index in Model 5.5.

Unfortunately, this approach introduces a new set of difficulties. In the first place, since Lazear's model refers implicitly to total labour compensation, it is hard to reconcile it specifically to the fact that fringes have exhibited higher growth rates than other labour costs (see Table 3.1). Firms are more likely to emphasise wage compensation in this type of model.

Secondly, if deferred fringes and current wages are simultaneously determined, then the causal mechanism implied in the Lazear model is less than clear-cut. Suppose, for example, that deferred fringes are paid systematically by firms principally as a result of collective bargaining pressures. In this event they may regard fringes as a necessarily incurred worker overhead payment in much the same way as search and training costs. In terms of Okun's analysis, deferred fringes may be discounted forward and regarded as part of toll payments. In a study of wage and non-wage benefits in the USA, Woodbury (1983) observes a negative relationship between the proportion of workers aged 16–34 within the total labour force and the wage share of total compensation. His main explanation for this is that some fringe benefits, and especially health and life insurance contributions, constitute fixed costs to the firm and so, being independent of wage levels, form a relatively high proportion of young workers' total compensation given their relatively low wages. Fringes, therefore, may account for a sizeable proportion of toll payments. In this case and following Okun's line of reasoning, fringes may feature as part of the determination of the seniority wage structure whereby workers in their earlier years pay for their share of the toll costs through lower wages. In the case of the quantitatively most important deferred fringe, private retirement benefits, Schiller and Weiss (1980) find support for this type of wage–fringe relationship in study of 133 large US firms. They conclude that 'younger workers bear a disproportionate share in the cost (in terms of reduced wages) of improved (private) retirement benefits' (p. 537). While this evidence fits Lazear's predictions, it nevertheless seems more (or at least *as*) compatible with a seniority-based wage structure designed to meet the costs of fixed investments.

A third problem with Lazear's agency model concerns a more general questionmark over one of its central predictions. Since younger workers receive compensation below their marginal products, Lazear argues that they will wish to work hours equivalent to their wage compensation rather than to the social value of time. This will tend to reduce their average hours relative to older workers where the opposite relationship between compensation and marginal product exists. Lazear goes on to argue that, as a corollary, 'old workers are more likely to accept overtime hours than are younger workers' (p. 617). While it is difficult to obtain longitudinal data with which to test these propositions, at least the European cross-sectional evidence points firmly against the predicted outcomes. In the UK, for example, both total weekly hours and overtime hours for dayworkers and shift-workers peak roughly in the middle of the 30–40 age group and fall off quite substantially between 40 and 65 (for an analysis, see National Board for Prices and Incomes, 1970, especially pp. 120–30).

10.3 WORKER PREFERENCES AND THE ROLE OF UNIONS

Several reasons have been offered as to why workers are likely to prefer a significant proportion of their total compensation in the form of fringe benefits (see, in particular, Rice, 1966; Lester, 1967; Freeman, 1981; Woodbury, 1983). Fringes are often taxed at lower marginal tax rates than equivalent compensation in wages. This is particularly true in the case of deferred fringes, such as pension plans, owing to a combination of factors. For example, Freeman (1981) points out that, in the USA, 'money placed into pension and related plans is not taxed when payment is first made, earns interest that is not taxed until paid out, is taxed at potentially favorable capital gains rates or as salary at lower income tax rates on retirement' (p. 495). This sort of relative advantage would be expected to exhibit itself in high income elasticities of demand for fringes as income growth moves workers into higher marginal tax brackets. However, irrespective of these tax advantages, as workers become older they are likely to want to substitute more deferred compensation for less current compensation (see Nealey, 1963), particularly in the areas of health and life insurance and retirement benefits. Woodbury's (1983) econometric estimates reveal elasticities of substitution between wages and retirement benefits to be significantly higher than between wages and health and life insurance, although all elasticities are well in excess of unity. Lester (1967) reports substantial growths in health and life insurance relative to wages in US company plans from 1945 to the mid-1960s. A related effect is that the fringe share of total compensation would be expected to be functionally related to the age composition of the workforce.

Preferences for fringes are perhaps better realised within fringe benefit schemes run by the firm rather than through private individual purchase. Insurance and other benefits bought through the firm may well be cheaper than the equivalent obtained by individuals owing to special rates for group purchase. Further, the degree of this firm-specific advantage would be expected to be positively related to firm size. As pointed out by Freeman (1981), large firms not only can spread the fixed costs of implementing and running deferred compensation schemes but also can expect to pay lower per-worker fees for management of the various funds. Further, the longer job tenure in larger firms due to greater possibilities for internal mobility should provide more encouragement about the worthwhileness of instigating and developing schemes. The evidence presented in Tables 3.5 and 3.7 is clearly in line with these predictions, as is that obtained by Woodbury (1983), who finds that the fringe share of total compensation is 3.0 to 3.5 percentage points higher in firms with more than 500 employees compared to those with fewer than 100 employees. However, notwithstanding economies through establishment size, Lester (1967) argues that, to many workers, the very fact that the firm takes over the individual need to search for suitable insurance cover, to accumulate funds to meet periodic premium payments and to process the necessary paper work provides in itself considerable advantages: 'The automatic character, convenience, and security of a company program are attractive features to persons on hourly pay' (p. 490).

Worker preferences combined with scale economies (as well as favourable corporate rates of taxation on fringes in several countries) are in themselves likely to encourage the firm to adopt some degree of fringe benefit compensation. This does not mean, however, that the potential selection and application of a given package of fringes that is perceived by the firm to be in its own best interests will coincide with the optimum choice of a typical worker. Indeed, any information the firm may elicit concerning individual worker preference might well be used to reduce the gap between the worker's optimum and minimum acceptable fringe benefit package thereby extracting some of the worker surplus. Given this line of argument, it would seem to follow that unionised workers may generally be in a better position to negotiate fringes than non-unionised workers (Freeman, 1976; Hirschman, 1976; Nelson, 1976). Workers combining collectively through a union can gauge more accurately the insurance needs and aspirations of individual members by collecting and evaluating relevant information. They are also in a better position to buy the expertise (of a comparable quality to that employed by management) with which to evaluate the prospects of and monitor the performance of funds that must be selected from a large complexity of available alternatives. Such expertise may also be used to judge the firm's own preferred strategy towards fringe compensation and so it can provide union negotiators with information, from the viewpoints of both sides, with which to strike effective bargains. Once collective agreements have been made, the union can then assess continually the resulting performance and associated actions of the firm. For example, it may wish to negotiate a long-term wage contract that is designed to rule out the possibility of the firm offsetting fringe costs by effecting compensating wage differentials. Also, following the possibility raised by Barnow and Ehrenberg (1979) concerning the growing cost of pensions with workers' age, it may seek to resist any attempt by the firm to 'encourage' high turnover among older workers.

Freeman's theoretical vehicle for introducing the role of unions into bargaining for fringe benefits is a median voter model. Unions are essentially political organisations and, in their desire to maximise members' support, they will tend to represent the preferences of older workers who have greater firm attachment. This contrasts with non-unionised sectors where firms might be expected to give more weight to the preferences of more mobile marginal workers (Freeman and Medoff, 1979). Since it has already been indicated that older workers have a relatively strong desire for compensation in the form of deferred fringe payments then, irrespective of other advantages of unions' bargaining for fringes, it would be expected that there would be more emphasis on fringe benefits agreements in unionised as opposed to non-unionised firms with a resulting higher proportion of total compensation in the form of fringes.[1] This latter expectation is strongly supported in the econometric evidence of Freeman (1981) and Woodbury (1983) and in the empirical evidence presented by Lester (1967).

There would seem to be real advantages to individual workers in combining collectively through a union in order to bargain for fringe benefits. That firms may respond to such collective representation is at least suggested by the evidence that fringes form a relatively high proportion of total compensation within unionised firms. It may be argued that in those firms that in any case display a preference for fringes – in order to protect specific human capital investments or to encourage higher productivity among younger workers – then this particular role of unions may be welcomed. However, since some doubt has already been cast on the strength of the human capital and agency models in explaining fringe payments, there may well be other reasons for firms' apparent greater acquiescence to individuals' fringe preferences expressed through the medium of a union. One possibility is that some unions are able to raise fringes above normal levels by exerting their monopoly power. Two other explanations are, perhaps, somewhat more generally convincing. Freeman and Medoff (1979) and others argue that the 'collective voice/institutional response' may well have positive effects on productivity through reducing quits, increasing worker morale and cooperation and improving worker–management communication. Viewed in this light, above-normal fringes may form part of the workers' share of the 'union increment' to productivity. The work of Duncan and Stafford (1980) provides a different type of explanation. They test the hypothesis that unions achieve wage differentials in recognition of the fact that, in general, unionised workers experience a relatively disadvantageous working environment.[2] The environment is such that it requires interdependent worker behaviour. Unions tend to represent workers who have less flexibility in their working hours and organisation and less control over the pace and scheduling of work. Relatively favourable reactions to workers' demands for fringes may be one means of achieving compensating differentials.[3]

The existing union bargaining models themselves stop well short of a complete explanation of the level of fringe benefit payments. Non-unionised firms too pay substantial fringe benefits (Leigh, 1981). Firms also pay fringes on a purely 'voluntary' basis outside the orbit of collective bargaining (see the examples in Tables 2.3 and 2.4). However, perhaps the strongest questionmark over the importance of this type of model arises from simple international comparisons of the ratio of fringes within total labour compensation and the degree of unionisation. The US has one of the smallest unionised sectors of all OECD countries and the FRG one of the largest and yet, as revealed under 'voluntary social welfare payments' in Table 3.1, the US fringe-ratio is over twice that of the FRG. Indeed, taking this particular comparison slightly further, this may admit a set of explanations of fringe benefit payments, not investigated here, that relate to individuals bargaining for wage compensation to cover major benefits excluded from, or inadequately covered by, statutory provision. Returning to Table 3.1, the relative standing of the US and FRG is reversed in the case of statutory social welfare. This relates to an argument raised by FitzRoy and Hart (1983) in a somewhat different context. Although unions are numerically much stronger in the FRG than in the US, they are *functionally* less important. In the FRG, a major body of social legislation (over health, pensions, short-time working, unemployment, etc.) has evolved that is strongly influenced by union representation, which has effectively surplanted part of the role played by unions in an earlier, more adversarial, climate of industrial relations. The absence of similar legislation in the US and, to a lesser extent, the UK may well account for their stronger emphasis on individual and union bargaining for equivalent insurance cover or alternative wage and non-wage compensation. In the extensive, though generally inconclusive, wage compensation literature (for a useful summary, see Brown, 1980) this particular avenue does not appear to have been explored.

10.4 A SIMULTANEITY PROBLEM

A reasonably complete explanation of why firms pay given levels of fringe benefits probably involves a combination of arguments taken from the three types of model outlined in sections 10.1–10.3. An unavoidable problem unfortunately arises when trying to establish the relative importance of each theoretical approach. In this chapter we have mentioned the human capital, agency and median voter models. All three involve arguments intimately tied up with long job tenure. In the human capital model, long tenure is desired by firms in order to recoup initial fixed labour investments. A compensation path that rises more steeply than marginal product encourages long tenure in the agency model. Long tenure is an attribute of the most influential union members in the median voter model. Discriminating among the models involves an inherent classical simultaneity problem given a possible two-way causality between size of fringe payments and length of tenure. The first two models suggest that causations runs from fringe level to tenure length, while the third model reverses the direction. Traditionally, it has been those researchers with an 'institutional' union approach who have had to take a defensive line over such problems (for a broader discussion of this point, see Freeman and Medoff, 1982). However, as indicated in sections 10.1 and 10.2, there are enough serious questionmarks over the adequacy of the other model constructs to predict fully the growth of fringes to leave at least considerable doubt over the outcomes of a comprehensive simultaneous equations approach.

10.5 FRINGE BENEFITS, MINIMUM WAGES AND HOURS OF WORK

Finally it is worth reporting briefly on another aspect of the relationship between fringe benefit and wage increases. Usually, this is investigated (or, more often, merely stated) in terms of increasing fringe growth inducing the firm to attempt offsetting reductions in the rate of wage growth. Recently, the problem has been examined in the opposite direction. Wessels (1980) has developed a model that predicts that an increase in minimum wages will, among other repercussions,[4] reduce per-worker fringe benefit compensation. A similar result is somewhat indirectly implied in work by Hashimoto (1982) on the relationship between minimum wages and on-the-job training. Hashimoto's theory and empirical evidence point towards minimum wage increases having an adverse effect on training, and so in the longer term, via the human capital model, deferred fringes may also be reduced given lower labour specificity. Both studies also report negative employment effects given minimum wage rises, but the main point of interest here is Wessel's claim that the firm is more likely to reduce its average working hours rather than its number of workers. Two reasons are given for this form of quantity-adjustment mode. First, hours reductions will avoid losses in specific capital. Second, given a cyclical/seasonal pattern of demand, firms can increase per-worker productivity by concentrating the hours reductions in slack periods. The problem with this conclusion is that, following the developments of the previous chapter, it overlooks the substitution of workers for hours following fringe decreases *given* that fringes contain large elements of fixed labour costs to the firm.[5] Overlooking scale effects and other complications, if Wessels is correct that minimum wage increases serve to reduce fringes, then the net effect on employment becomes an interesting, and open, empirical question.

NOTES

1 This line of argument is strengthened when it is considered that the degree of unionisation is related positively to firm size (see Tables 3.8 and 3.9). Longer

average job tenure in larger firms (especially in the case of Japan) would serve to reinforce the union influence on deferred fringes through the median voter representation.

2 Duncan and Stafford recognise that two structural hypotheses are consistent with the association between unionism and conditions of work. The first specifies that unionism is a function of the working conditions, while the second specifies that the working conditions represent a response by employers to unionism.

3 Since these arguments would be expected to apply more to manual than non-manual workers, the fact that it is the latter group that receives the higher proportion of fringes (see Table 3.4) perhaps limits the forcefulness of this line of explanation.

4 In fact Wessel's main interest is in the effects of minimum wage increases on quit rates and participation rates in the presence of fringe benefit compensation.

5 Actually there may be an offsetting increase in fixed costs since Wessel's model predicts a short-run increase in quit rates following a minimum wage increase. Through (5.5) this will serve to increase the value of non-recurring fixed NWLCs.

REFERENCES

Barnow, B. S. and R. G. Ehrenberg (1979), 'The costs of defined benefit pension plans and firm adjustments', *The Quarterly Journal of Economics*, 94, 523–540.

Becker, G. S. (1964), *Human Capital: A Theoretical and Empirical Analysis, with Special Reference to Education*, New York, NY: National Bureau of Economic Research.

Becker, G. S. and G. Stigler (1974), 'Law enforcement, malfeasance and compensation', *Journal of Legal Studies*, 3, 1–18.

Brown, C. (1980), 'Equalizing differences in the labour market', *The Quarterly Journal of Economics*, 94, 113–134.

Duncan, G. J. and F. R. Stafford (1980), 'Do union members receive compensating wage differentials?', *American Economic Review*, 70, 355–371.

FitzRoy, F. R. and R. A. Hart (1983), 'Hours of work, layoffs and unemployment insurance: theory and practice in an international perspective', Berlin: International Institute of Management, mimeo.

Freeman, R. B. (1976), 'Individual mobility and union voice in the labor market', *American Economic Review* (Proceedings), 66, 361–368.

Freeman, R. B. (1981), 'The effect of unionism on fringe benefits', *Industrial and Labor Relations Review*, 34, 489–509.

Freeman, R. B. and J. L. Medoff (1979), 'The two faces of unionism', *The Public Interest*, 57, 69–93.

Freeman, R. B. and J. L. Medoff (1982), 'The impact of collective bargaining: can the new facts be explained by monopoly unionism?', *National Bureau of Economic Research*, Cambridge, Mass: Working Paper No 837.

Hashimoto, M. (1981), 'Firm-specific human capital as a shared investment', *American Economic Review*, 71, 475–482.

Hashimoto, M. (1982), 'Minimum wage effects on training on the job', *American Economic Review*, 72, 1070–1087.

Hirschman, A. O. (1976), 'Some uses of the exit-voice approach – discussion', *American Economic Review* (Proceedings), 66, 386–389.

Lazear, E. P. (1981), 'Agency, earnings profiles, productivity, and hours restrictions', *American Economic Review*, 71, 606–620.

Leigh, D. E. (1981), 'The effects of unionism on workers' valuation of future pension benefits', *Industrial and Labor Relations Review*, 34, 510–521.

Lester, R. A. (1967), 'Benefits as a preferred form of compensation', *Southern Economic Journal*, 33, 488–495.

Medoff, J. L. and K. G. Abraham (1980), 'Experience, performance, and earnings', *The Quarterly Journal of Economics*, 95, 703–736.

National Board for Prices and Incomes (1970), *Hours of Work, Overtime and Shiftworking*, Report No. 161, London: HMSO.

Nealey, M. (1963), 'Pay and benefit preference', *Industrial Relations*, 3, 17–28.

Nelson, R. L. (1976), 'Some uses of the exit-voice – discussion', *American Economic Review* (Proceedings), 66, 389–391.

Parsons, D. O. (1972), 'Specific human capital: an application to quit rates and layoff rates', *Journal of Political Economy*, 80, 1120–1143.

Rice, R. (1966), 'Skill, earnings and the growth of wage supplements', *American Economic Review* (Proceedings), 54, 583–593.

Schiller, B. R. and R. D. Weiss (1980), 'Pensions and wages: a test for equalizing differences', *The Review of Economics and Statistics*, 62, 529–538.

Wessels, W. J. (1980), 'The effect of minimum wages in the presence of fringe benefits: an expanded model', *Economic Inquiry*, 18, 293–313.

Woodbury, S. A. (1983), 'Substitution between wage and nonwage benefits', *American Economic Review*, 73, 166–182.

11 Should Governments Attempt to Reduce Non-Wage Labour Costs?

From the information presented in the first three chapters it is clear that, throughout most OECD countries, non-wage labour costs form a large and growing proportion of the average firm's total expenditure on labour. Further, it is reasonable to infer from Table 3.2 that, in many of these countries, the real growth of the costs has outstripped real productivity growth. For two broad types of reason, there would appear to be strong arguments in support of government policies designed to reduce the costs, especially within an era marked by record postwar unemployment rates.

In the first place, as we have seen at a number of earlier points, cutbacks in certain types of costs may stimulate new employment. Reductions in costs might not only help to produce beneficial scale effects on firms' output and employment but also, insofar as the cost reductions can be targeted towards lowering the proportion of labour fixity, employment may be stimulated through the workers–hours substitution channel.

Secondly, government anti-inflation policies that are geared to keep real wage growth in line with real growth of GNP may be seriously undermined if, effectively, labour can substitute out of wage payments and into fringe benefits as a means of circumventing direct and indirect controls. Notwithstanding these possibilities, a highly cautious approach is called for when making policy recommendations with respect to cost reductions since, as with almost any other area of government policy, evaluation of the net impact of government action is confronted with several complications and uncertainties.

Statutorily imposed social welfare costs are the most obvious area for government policy initiatives. The first point to establish concerns the long-run repercussions of cost reductions. Any significant cut in payroll taxes would almost certainly constitute a redistribution of the tax burden from employers to workers. It would seem impracticable to envisage that, in any significant sense, governments are politically able to accompany tax cuts with reductions in their short- and medium-term obligations to the retired, the unemployed and the sick. In fact, even if it were feasible to reduce retirement pensions and unemployment benefits, governments may still have to face, especially in the case of pensions, increased obligations for the simple exogenous reason that the sizes of the population cohorts concerned are growing relative to the total economically active population. Given this general constraint, it is difficult to envisage that the *long-run* outcomes following cost reductions to firms would differ significantly from a policy of 'no action'. If, as seems likely, government reductions in payroll tax burdens to firms are offset by increases in employee contributions and/or other forms of individual taxation, then final outcomes would differ little from firms' own long-term abilities to shift taxes on to their workers through backward and forward tax shifting.

Within a shorter time perspective, government cutbacks in statutory NWLCs might reasonably be anticipated to exert a greater influence on firms' employment strategies. However, the developments in Chapter 9 point to considerable uncertainties about net outcomes. For example, possible beneficial scale effects on employment may well be offset by opposing substitution effects given the prevailing payroll tax structure. Even where fixed worker costs can be reduced, the very uneven incidence of fixity – across industries, between sexes and over occupational skill groups (see Chapters 2 and 3) – provides real difficulties in ascertaining whether the work places so created would match adequately the job requirements of the unemployed.

Given these and other complications, only two types of policy initiative seem to be worth exploring further based on the analysis in Chapter 9. The first involves the provision of subsidies to the firm's statutory NWLCs (or, even, direct wages) for *net additions* to its workforce. It is argued in Chapter 9 that this type of government intervention would be expected to be a more effective, and certainly a less ambiguous, means of generating new jobs compared to equivalent general wage and non-wage subsidies. This offers a potentially fruitful policy outlet to governments operating under tight constraints on public expenditure increases. Within a macro context, there may well be net advantages in *transferring* resources from existing 'blanket' subsidy schemes – designed to preserve jobs in, for example, declining industries or problematic geographical locations – to marginal subsidy programmes designed to encourage additional employment growth within relatively buoyant firms. However, from the analysis and performance of this type of scheme under the French solidarity contracts (see section 9.2), it seems likely that the imposition of additional conditions for receiving such subsidies, such as reducing existing average working hours, will serve merely to detract from their full employment-creating potential. With a much greater questionmark over its efficacy, the second type of policy involves the complete removal of earnings ceiling limits to statutory welfare payroll taxes.

To the extent that such action helps to reduce labour fixity, then some employment creation may be stimulated. As discussed in section 9.4, however, a firm conclusion in this direction can only be reached subject to a number of other considerations that serve generally to offset the employment impact.

As always, it should be emphasised that governments are not able costlessly to effect such changes and, in the absence of a general equilibrium framework, full macro implications cannot be ascertained. These policies gain some support only with respect to the partial approach adopted here. In any case, even if outcomes remain the same within a fuller analysis, it is doubtful whether the overall impact on employment arising from these measures would be other than relatively small.

In the area of unemployment insurance and related social welfare contributions, there has been recent pressure on governments, particularly from employers' associations in several European countries, to reduce payroll taxes. This has accompanied a growing interest by governments in examining the supply-side effects of cuts in benefits. The assessment of a policy that involves *both* contribution and benefit rate reductions, itself attractive where self-financing is an objective, involves unravelling a number of simultaneously determined employment responses. The main objective of Chapter 8 is to stress the fact that too little attention has been given to the demand-side effects of changes in obligatory contributions. These may or may not serve to reinforce the labour market outcomes of changes in supply-side variables and certainly they need to be accommodated as a precondition for evaluating supply effects.

Governments may also attempt to reduce firms' private expenditures on non-wages by fiscal methods. Obvious examples here are increases in both corporate and individual marginal tax rates on fringe benefits to levels comparable with rates of taxation on direct labour compensation. Corporate tax increases would be expected to have a direct negative effect on firms' willingness to pay fringes, while individual tax increases would be expected to reduce the supply pressures on firms to raise the proportion of the fringe benefits within total compensation. Not only might such a policy have the effect of reducing labour fixity, thereby stimulating employment, but it may also be deemed to have wider positive welfare implications. Large variations in the levels of fringe compensation due to such factors as firm size, union strength, skill group and sex are probably one of the important factors associated with labour market segmentation. Primary markets with both relatively low turnover rates and stable wage paths might be expected to correlate quite highly with the general level of fixity of the workforce and, in particular, with the level of fringe benefit compensation. In the case of secondary markets the converse is true, with generally highly unstable employment and wages accompanying relatively low levels of fixity and fringe benefits.

From the empirical literature, there can be little doubt that favourable rates of taxation form an important reason for firms' and workers' preferences for fringes. However, before deciding whether and by what amount taxes should be raised, it is first important to be clear about the precise motivations behind fringe benefit compensation. If, for example, firms pay fringes mainly because of a desire to protect human capital investments, then a policy of increasing taxes may not be as advisable as in other situations. Firms invest in the specific human capital of their workers in order to improve marginal products. A reason for paying fringes in general, and deferred fringes in particular, may be to ensure an adequate return on such investment by discouraging high turnover rates among workers. If favourable marginal tax rates play some part in encouraging workers for their part to accept such benefits in place of their equivalent amount in wages, then indirectly the returns to the forgone taxes may be regarded in terms of the reinforced willingness of firms to undertake productivity-enhancing specific investments. However, it has been argued in Chapter 10 that the human capital story falls well short of providing an adequate or complete explanation for the motivation behind fringe payments. The role of individual preferences in its own right, often expressed collectively through a union, would appear to be highly influential in determining the level of fringe benefit compensation. To the extent that unions achieve above-normal levels of fringes through the exercise of monopoly power, then the welfare case for fringe benefit tax increases may be relatively persuasive. On the other hand, this line of argument is not so appealing in cases where unions may serve to enhance the firm's productivity through representation by collective voice or where fringes are used to compensate union workers for adverse working conditions.

There is indirect evidence, however, that may point towards support for some degree of marginal tax increases on fringes. While significant average national *levels* of fringe benefits may, in large part, be explained by economic arguments that suggest productive returns to fringe payments, it is not so easy to account in the same way for the recent *growth rates* in non-obligatory NWLCs in the UK, USA (see Table 3.1) and other countries. Given the number of recessionary years within the time-period covered in Table 3.1, it is difficult to reconcile UK and US growth paths with significant increases in average per capita human capital investments and, even more so, with a growth in union influence. This may well suggest that much of the net increase in non-obligatory contributions during this time has resulted from the ability of certain groups within an imperfectly functioning labour market to offset the effects of anti-inflationary wages policies by a switch in emphasis towards remuneration in the form of fringe benefits. Also, the achievement of an increased proportion of total compensation in the form of fringes may have proved an effective method of counteracting increases in effective income tax rates, which have occurred owing to the failure of governments to adjust marginal tax rates sufficiently to account for the tax effects of wage inflation. To this extent, at least, there may well be a strong case for tightening fiscal controls.

The ability of governments to reduce labour fixity through redistributing the payroll tax burden or by increasing tax rates on fringes may produce the benefit of increased average employment levels over the cycle. From both workers' and governments' viewpoints there is an important offsetting cost consideration in this strategy. In times of recession, firms may well be less inclined to hoard labour, which represents a higher variable factor input. From the evidence presented in Chapter 6, we may conclude that fixed worker costs to the firm act as a cyclically stabilising mechanism for employment in much the same way as income taxes act to stabilise the national income in the face of cyclical fluctuations in investment. Relative employment stability is also a feature of high labour fixity as emphasised in the discussion of wage flexibility in section 7.2. Higher specific labour investments increase the likelihood of a price, rather than quantity, means of adjustment in the face of economic fluctuations. Herein lies the nature of a fundamental policy trade-off between employment and labour fixity. Lower labour fixity may mean more employment over the cycle but cyclically less stable employment; greater fixity means less employment but greater employment security. Assessing the optimum point on the trade-off is not an easy task.

Index